W9-AVH-392

Living & Working in
London

Books to change your life and work.
Accessible, easy to read and easy to act on –
other titles in the *How To* series include:

Finding Voluntary Work Abroad
All the information you need for getting valuable work experience overseas

Teaching Abroad
How and where to find teaching and lecturing jobs worldwide

Getting a Job in Europe
How to find short or long-term employment throughout Europe

Spending a Year Abroad
A guide to opportunities for self-development and discovery around the world

How to Find a Temporary Job Abroad
A world of opportunities for everyone

The *How To series* now contains
around 200 titles in the following categories:

Business & Management
Career Choices
Career Development
Computers & the Net
Creative Writing
Home & Family
Living & Working Abroad
Personal Development
Personal Finance
Self-Employment & Small Business
Study Skills & Student Guides

For full details, please send to our distributors for a free copy of the latest catalogue:

How To Books
Customer Services Dept.
Plymbridge Distributors Ltd, Estover Road
Plymouth PL6 7PZ, United Kingdom
Tel: 01752 202301   Fax: 01752 202331
http://www.howtobooks.co.uk

Living & Working in

London

*All you need to know
to enjoy this capital city*

JOANNA MINETT

How To Books

Dedicated to June Peschkes
Thank you for your encouragement

Published by How To Books Ltd,
3 Newtec Place, Magdalen Road,
Oxford OX4 1RE. United Kingdom.
Tel: (01865) 793806. Fax: (01865) 248780.
email: info@howtobooks.co.uk
http://www.howtobooks.co.uk

All rights reserved. No part of this work may be reproduced
or stored in an information retrieval system (other than for
purposes of review) without the express permission of the
publisher in writing.

© Copyright 2000 Joanna Minett

First published 2000
Reprinted 2000

British Library Cataloguing in Publication Data.
A catalogue record for this book is available from
the British Library.

Edited by Sarah Hudson
Cover design by Shireen Nathoo Design
Cover image by PhotoDisc
Cover copy by Sallyann Sheridan

Produced for How To Books by Deer Park Productions
Typeset by PDQ Typesetting, Newcastle-under-Lyme, Staffs.
Printed and bound by Cromwell Press, Trowbridge, Wiltshire

NOTE: The material contained in this book is set out in good
faith for general guidance and no liability can be accepted
for loss or expense incurred as a result of relying in particular
circumstances on statements made in the book. Laws and
regulations are complex and liable to change, and readers should
check the current position with the relevant authorities before
making personal arrangements.

Contents

List of Illustrations

1

Introducing London

London is the capital city of Great Britain. It is situated in the south east of England and lies astride the River Thames. The notorious M25, approximately 20 miles from its centre, surrounds it and has improved access in recent years.

HISTORY AND BACKGROUND

Many people who choose to live in London have little knowledge of the history of this great city. The majority of its 7 million yearly visitors, be they long term or short term, gain only a superficial impression as they pass through. They visit places such as: the British Museum, the National Gallery, Oxford Street, Westminster Abbey, Madame Tussaud's, theatre shows and the Tower of London and while these are all excellent places to visit you will gain only a limited knowledge of London's special character. There is so much more depth and feeling to London.

History

Originally called *Londinium*, London has historically developed and grown from three distinct centres:

1. A walled settlement, founded by the Romans on the banks of the Thames in the first century AD. This area is now known as the 'City' or the 'Square Mile' which is the centre of the banking and finance sector of London and Europe – some might even say the world.

2. The south bank, just across the river from the City, now known as Southwark. It was the original site for monasteries, hospitals, inns, fairs and pleasure buildings.

3. Abbey Royal Palace, which was built in 1703 one mile upstream in Westminster, now Buckingham Palace.

There have been many rebuilding exercises throughout the years – too many to detail. World wars, bombings and fires have devastated much of the original architecture. However, when walking around the capital you can still see amazing original architecture and structures. Two of the most major destructive events in London were:

- the Great Fire of 1666 which burned for four whole days in the 'City' destroying everything in its path

- the Blitz, which saw almost continuous bombing from September 1940 to May 1941 with masses of homes destroyed, leaving 155,000 families homeless and no gas or electricity supplies remaining connected throughout the capital.

As a consequence, London is accustomed to rebuilding work and has historically responded well under this type of pressure. Londoners pride themselves on their resilience. This could be seen, more recently, from the local reaction to the IRA bomb in the City in 1992. The following Monday morning employees of financial institutions were operating from mobile caravans to continue trading and keep their reputations intact.

Background
The population of Central London has now levelled out to between 6 and 7 million although Greater London includes a further 6 million. It has two strategic land features:

- the M25, London's orbital motorway which was finally completed in 1987 and was quickly overloaded by traffic

- the Green Belt area (created in the 1930s) covers 55 square miles of countryside just inside the M25; development of this land is prohibited.

Many people have moved out of London in recent years to seek:

- cleaner and fresher air; levels of pollution are currently at an all-time high even though major steps are now being taken to improve it

- better value-for-money housing; within the capital most people live in apartments, often without gardens

- a slower pace of life; the fast pace can become tiring and distressing

- cheaper living costs.

One of the primary reasons for London's individuality is that it has always been the one city in the western world which has fulfilled every urban function:

- shipping
- commerce
- finance
- base for royalty
- law
- government headquarters

The amount of destruction over the centuries has led to a totally haphazard rebuilding plan. Many people consider that this adds to its overall idiosyncratic charm. Others feel that even if this is the case it is time for building, planning and transport to be under the control of one body; they feel that London needs its own voice.

The government has never taken overall responsibility for London and as a consequence the planning and development has little structure or form. It has delegated this responsibility to the numerous London boroughs which have separate councils and differing amounts of government funding and different views on what is needed. Also, historically the councils have been run by different political parties. Little or no cohesion has existed between them.

At various times there has been an overall council responsible for London. Until recently the most famous was the Greater London Council (GLC), which was disbanded by the Conservative government under Margaret Thatcher. Traditionally the ruling government has always wanted to keep some level of control over London. As a consequence full power has never been delegated to a London Council.

London now has a new Mayor, Ken Livingstone. He is remembered for his previous leadership of the GLC and his reduction of travel costs.

Because he lives in London the people consider he will keep their interests in mind. His position as Mayor has made him the second most powerful leader in the country.

UNDERSTANDING THE POLITICAL STRUCTURE

Whilst the position of London is straightforward, the internal political structure is more difficult to understand. As already mentioned, there are a variety of boroughs in and around London which are responsible in a similar way to other councils around the country. These will remain in place even under a main London council.

As you travel around the capital you will notice many changes as you move from one borough to another. These changes may include:

- the level of cleanliness on the streets
- the number and types of rubbish bins available
- the quality of healthcare available
- whether parking permits are needed and at what cost
- the amount and level of all local facilities.

In addition to these, the amount of council tax payable differs enormously from one borough to another, as does the competence level of schools.

ESSENTIAL INFORMATION

When moving to London there is a whole host of books, leaflets and information which you can buy or obtain free to assist you. The Further Reading section at the end of this book gives more details. This information falls into three distinct categories:

1. Essential.
2. Useful but not essential.
3. Nice to have.

The main focus at this stage will be on that which is essential for you to obtain at the beginning of your move:

- a map of London streets. The most popular street guide is the *A–Z of London*, although Nicholson's *Streetfinder* is an alternative and shows one-way streets
- an underground 'tube' map (available free from tube stations)
- local bus map (available free from bus stations and local newsagents)
- details of transport costs (available free from tube stations)
- details of relevant council districts (available free – look up details in a local telephone directory)
- local doctors, schools etc. (consult the London telephone

directory – available at a local library).

It is a good idea to telephone and arrange for the information to be posted to you prior to your move. As you review it, here are some points to bear in mind:

- costs of different types of transport
- varying amounts of council tax payable
- reports on schools and healthcare
- convenience of locations to main transport schemes, particularly main-line train terminals.

The more information you collect and read prior to your move, the easier and smoother things are likely to go.

UNDERSTANDING THE LEGAL REQUIREMENTS

If you have a British passport there are no special legal requirements to moving to London.

However, if you are arriving from overseas you need to bear in mind that the United Kingdom immigration regulations are complex and professional advice may be needed. If you wish to enter the country on a permanent basis you may well need to have a convincing argument.

However, work visas and other documents can sometimes be procured easily.

Any reputable lawyer or consultant will assess feasibility and normally only assist you if there is a good chance of success.

Citizens of member countries of the European Union
If you are a citizen of a member country of the European Union there are no barriers to working in other member states. Contact the British Embassy in your own country for help and useful advice.

Citizens from countries outside the European Union
Contact the British Embassy in your own country and a reputable lawyer. Choose a lawyer who offers the following assistance as well as excellent legal advice:

- offices convenient to London

- full tax advice
- employment advice
- an understanding of the business sectors throughout London
- investment advice
- an understanding of the pension systems in both countries
- assistance with finding accommodation even if only on a temporary basis.

Cost will vary according to whether you want a temporary or permanent visa and citizenship rather than a resident's permit. Remember to include these costs when you review your finances.

REVIEWING FINANCES

Your move may be constrained by your financial situation. At the very least you will need to plan and budget carefully before embarking on the move. You should take time and care over the financial aspects. It will save you getting into difficult situations later on.

Understanding the costs
Costs for any move can escalate from the initial estimates. If you budget carefully you will be able to keep costs to a minimum. At each stage you will need to make accurate estimates and double-check your costings. (See *Planning your finances*, page 15).

Banking and finance
Throughout London you will find a branch of most banks, including overseas banks. If you have always kept your bank account at your home town in Great Britain you may decide to leave it there. However, you can always transfer it to a London branch of the same bank. This is easy and should be a painless exercise.

From overseas, you will probably find a branch of your own bank within the 'City'. In this situation it is advisable to open an account as soon as possible, otherwise you could begin to lose money on any currency fluctuations.

In the cashless society of today it is never essential to have your branch on your doorstep as you will find numerous cashpoint (hole-in-the-wall) machines. It may not be a priority item to sort out but there are some points to consider when making your decision.

Advantages of moving your account to London
- A London bank manager may well understand the plights of moving to London and the drain on finances to a greater extent than your local bank manager.

- You may feel more comfortable having your account local to where you live.

Disadvantages to moving your account to London
- You may receive a less personal service than leaving your account with a bank manager who has known you all his or her life.

- Most of the main high street banks in London have administration centres on the outskirts or even outside the capital which can lead to confusion.

- You will need to begin to build relationships with bank officials from scratch.

Planning your finances

One of the most difficult aspects of any move is to estimate your costs. Here is a guide of possible costs to work from. Everyone's move is different, so it is not a definitive list, but takes into account most situations. For each item you may need to take advice on how much it could add up to.

1. Travel and transportation to your new home.

2. Connection charges for any of the utilities (gas, electricity, telephone).

3. Deposit on rental accommodation or purchase deposit, if buying.

4. At least one month's rent in advance.

5. Fees for registration with estate agents.

6. If buying property; fees for lawyers, surveyor, etc.

7. Travel costs to view properties and search for a job.

8. Cost of a parking permit.

9. Any new clothes needed for interviews etc.

10. Food to see you through before you receive your first salary payment.

11. Visa and immigration costs.

You need to remember that all of these costs need to be paid before you receive any income. One cost which can easily escalate is travel.

Reducing costs

Here are a few hints and tips to help you to keep your costs to a minimum:

1. Undertake the move yourself, as the hiring of a removal company can prove extremely expensive.

2. Seek out estate agents which have no registration fees for tenants looking to rent.

3. If you are viewing a lot of properties try to arrange the appointments all on one day, so that you can benefit from a one-day Travelcard. Even better, persuade the estate agent to take you round.

4. Use local papers to look for properties. They may cost less as the vendor or landlord has fewer outgoings (no estate agent's fees).

5. Go the local library to look through the papers so you do not have to buy them.

6. Seek the assistance of parents or guardians for deposits to utilities as many of these companies will accept a guarantee from a parent instead of a payment.

CHECKLIST

1. Assess your financial situation and estimate the costs of a move.

2. Seek out legal advice and visit the British Embassy in your country if visiting from overseas.

3. Find your local library and read the local papers and any others with properties for sale or rent.

4. Buy a London street map.

5. Collect information on council districts, schools and healthcare.

2

Organising the Move

Once you have made your decision to move to London keep in mind what a major step you are undertaking. It can be stressful. A larger number of factors need to be considered and thought should be given to:

- Making the move go as easily and smoothly as possible.

- Keeping costs to a minimum.

- Keeping control of the situation.

- Seeking out help and advice as needed.

- Timing the move carefully.

If you spend time planning and organising the move you will be rewarded in the longer term with a smooth, low-cost move.

PLANNING THE MOVE

Moving to London will require more flexibility than moving to many other locations. Each situation is different and the next two chapters give the foundation for structuring and planning the move.

Where to start

It is always difficult to know where to start with such a move. Do you find suitable accommodation first or an appropriate job first? This will most likely be dictated by individual circumstances.

If you live outside London, it is exceptionally difficult to find suitable accommodation to fit your needs and price-range in London. Most of the better properties, whether they are flat-shares, rentals or purchases, disappear quickly. You need to be able to view the property and make your decision with a few days.

If you can, ask a friend to help you out with somewhere to stay while you look around. It will improve your chances of finding a more suitable place to live. Alternatively many companies, when transferring people to London, will assist the move by providing temporary accommodation – take up their offer.

The following will be useful to have on you at all times:

- . Two notebooks – one for the house move and one for the job search. Keep all information noted, including names and addresses, telephone numbers and dates.

- Your London A–Z street map, local bus map and tube map.

- Loose change for tubes, buses and telephone (or your mobile phone fully charged).

Useful assistance

There are several publications and a multitude of information written about London. Much of it is aimed at the tourist industry. However, it will still give you a valuable insight into areas to live and finding your way around. Read as much as possible. Obtain as many opinions as possible.

Always remember that you can talk to ten people who live in London and receive ten different views on any district or area. Many people, when they first move, find themselves living in an area by pure chance. This may prove satisfactory, but there are many things which can be done to ensure that you are happy with your chosen location.

Other help and advice can be gained from:

- country-wide estate agents; although probably only a second-hand knowledge

- work colleagues or fellow students; talk to as many people as possible to get as many views as you can

- reading the *Evening Standard*; published Monday to Friday afternoon in London

- watching the local London news on television and listening to local radio stations

- London estate agents, who are always convinced that the area they live in is the best.

Timetable

Structuring a realistic, working timetable will assist you. It gives you a focus and an idea of how long it should take to get moved. A suggestion for a possible timetable if you are looking to rent or flat-share could be:

Week 1 Visit areas; decide which areas to focus on.

Week 2 Continue to visit areas; see estate agents; read local press.

Week 3 Visit specific properties; make a decision.

Week 4 Landlord takes references. Arrange move; organise utilities; sort out finance.

Week 5 Move in.

If you are looking to buy a property weeks 1–3 may be similar but your decision may take longer and the actual move will definitely be slower. (See *Finding accommodation* on page 28.)

Moving house and moving job are known respectively to be two of the most stressful life-events. Combining the two means doubling the stress. This will be increased five-fold when moving to London, because, even if you have lived in a city before, you will find the pace faster and attitudes more aggressive. The most anxiety is likely to be if the move is from overseas, particularly if English is your second language.

As the move progresses you will need to be aware of how stress affects you. It usually comes in three phases:

1. Alarm: most of your energy is spent panicking that it cannot possibly be done.

2. Resistance: you are at the point where you do not want to have to do it, so consequently you do not put all of your energies into the move.

3. Exhaustion: you become ill because you are so worried and concerned about the move.

Part of your overall plan to move must include a regime to combat stress. Look after yourself by eating well and taking regular exercise. Discuss your feelings with a friend or relative; someone who has been through a similar experience. Keep a positive attitude. More ways to avoid stress are detailed in Chapter 4.

DECIDING WHERE TO LIVE

A map of London will give you an indication of the size and location of some of the main districts. You will find that it will not take long before you understand the basic geographical structure.

London postal districts are straightforward. The lower the number the closer the district is to the centre of London. Thus:

- W9 means west 9 in west London, further out from the centre than W1.

- E17 means east 17 in east London.

- SW6 means south west 6, closer in than SW16.

If you have the whole of London to choose from, the choice could be made easier. Here are some factors which need to be taken into account:

- types of transport and distance of property from any main-line stations, airports, etc. which you may need to use

- convenience to shops

- any known friends or relatives in the area

- proximity to study or work location

- price range

- safety aspects for walking around alone, especially for women at night

- council tax rates, which can vary even from street to street in some areas

- preferred style of living environment.

Visiting areas

After reading about and researching your chosen areas you will need to spend some time visiting them to decide where you would like to live. This will prove to be both an interesting and frustrating experience. You may well find a suitable district but no accommodation is available within your price range. Conversely you may find a lovely flat but the area is totally unsuitable. Be patient.

You need to choose an area where you feel comfortable and where you believe you can live for the duration of the tenancy you sign, or until you sell the property, if you buy.

1. Visit the area during daylight and darkness. It is logical to walk around during both, especially to and from any local tube stations. Look around you, take in the atmosphere, walk into a local pub or bar on your own to test friendliness.

2. Investigate how easy it is to get a taxi to and from the area. There are certain areas where London taxis will not go. This exercise will also give you the exact cost of such transport.

3. Visit at weekends. You may find that there is a football stadium or concert hall close to where you want to live which causes noise and disturbance.

4. Visit the area on a rainy day. Everywhere looks nice on a sunny day!

5. Go to a local restaurant to see how the service is and what attitudes are like.

6. Talk to local shop owners or restaurant owners to get a feel of what they think the area is like.

7. Walk the full length of different roads because areas in London can change dramatically within a short distance.

DECIDING WHERE TO WORK

Where you work can be dictated by the type of job you are seeking. If this is the case then it is essential to choose your accommodation to fit in with your work.

However, if you do have a choice and want to keep your commuting time to a minimum, here are some hints and tips:

- choose a work location where you only need to take one form of transport to and from home and do not have to change tube lines or buses

- investigate the reliability of the local tube lines and bus routes as these vary tremendously from district to district

- consider working within walking distance of your new home by giving yourself a sensible radius and exploring the companies within that radius

- buy all local papers published in the area
- visit local job centres, even if it is just to get an idea of job availability and salary within the area
- consider the possibility of seasonal or temporary work if it keeps you close to home.

CONSIDERING COMMUTING

Commuting is a fact of life in and around London. The majority of people take over 45 minutes to get to work, even when living in the capital. It is something which you will need to get used to. There are some basic rules about commuting in rush hour which, although not law, are strictly adhered to by most commuters:

- A very London characteristic is not to talk to unknown travellers during a journey. If you choose to do so, you'll probably be regarded as rather odd!
- Always stand on the right side of both the up and down escalators. The left side is for those people who wish to walk or run up and down. You will be the most unpopular person in the rush hour if you hold everyone up. Whilst initially this may seem odd, you will find that within a few weeks you will be feeling exactly the same thing!
- Follow the notices in the underground system at all times; for example, where it is stated which side of the corridor you should walk on. Again, it is to keep the mass of people moving along smoothly.
- There are dedicated seats for disabled and/or elderly people in the underground carriages and buses. By all means use one but be prepared to give it up should a person need it more than you.
- Obey the no-smoking signs. All of London Transport is now a no-smoking area.
- There is no queuing system to get onto the underground carriages, so be prepared to push and barge your way on. However, always let passengers off before getting on.
- At bus stops there is usually a queue. Although it is not always clear which queue is for which bus; practice will make perfect.

There is a very strict queueing system for the Waterloo & City Line 'The Drain' – as it better known, a name coined from the days when it was a large drain! It is the direct link between Waterloo station and Bank station for the City. You must stand in the queue and follow the person in front of you onto the train. The platforms are clearly marked with solid white lines where the doors will open. Any deviance from this causes abuse and aggression from fellow passengers. So be warned!

Rush hours are from 07.30–09.30 and from 16.30–18.30. Although there will be more trains at these times the journey is likely to take longer. This is because the trains are kept in the stations longer as more people will be getting on and off. The start of rush hour is usually the fastest time to travel.

Making the most out of commuting

If you do end up having a long commuting time, there are certain things which can be done to make the most of it:

- read newspapers and magazines to keep yourself up to date with the news or gossip
- choose to study
- read interesting novels
- meditate – be careful not to miss your stop, though
- catch up on sleep.

PREPARING TO MOVE HOME

The more prepared you are, the easier the move will be. Here is a checklist of things you need to consider:

- packaging and transportation of your belongings (do not forget that you too will need transport)
- any assistance which may be needed on arrival at your destination
- discussion with advisers on immigration to ensure that all paperwork is completed in time
- financial awareness of costs to ensure that you are covered

- all relevant documentation signed and delivered
- all relevant parties notified of change of address and telephone number
- insurance arranged.

ARRIVING IN LONDON

At last, the day has arrived for you to move into your new residence. How you will arrive will be dependent on two factors:

- where you are coming from
- the amount of possessions you have to move.

If you have only clothes and a few smaller items you may be able to make the move conveniently on public transport. This will save on costs even though you may find it tiring and cumbersome. Transporting even the smallest of cases around the underground system can be hazardous and difficult. It is bound to be that one day when the up-escalators have stopped working.

Airports

The main London airport is Heathrow (LHR), which is 15 miles west. Gatwick (LGW), the second airport, is situated 27 miles south of London. In addition there are two other airports: London City (10 miles east), which handles European business flights mainly, and Stansted (37 miles north) which handles international flights and is fast developing as the airport for cut-price flights to all over the world. Heathrow and Gatwick handle by far the most international flights and both have easy and convenient transport into central London.

Arriving from Heathrow

There is a direct service by train from Heathrow to Paddington station, which takes 15 minutes and leaves every 15 minutes. It is quite an expensive option. The underground also goes direct to and from central London (Piccadilly Circus) to Heathrow via the Piccadilly line. The underground is much cheaper than the train, but it can take up to 90 minutes. If your destination is west London the underground may prove to be the most sensible form of transport.

Coaches and buses (Airbus A1 and A2) run regularly from the

airport throughout the day and night. Again, if your destination is west London this will prove convenient, otherwise the end of the journey is Victoria coach station and you will have to organise the remainder of the journey from there.

Black taxis and local taxi services are available from Heathrow to London and the surrounding area (around £40 to central London). There is a black taxi rank where you can queue, although other taxi services will need to be pre-ordered.

Arriving from Gatwick
The Victoria to Gatwick Express train runs every 15 minutes during the day and every 30 minutes during the night. The journey takes approximately 30 minutes.

In addition, there is a regular bus service (Flightline 777) to Victoria coach station throughout the day and night.

There is no black taxi rank at Gatwick, but local taxi services are available (around £40 to central London). Ask at the information desk.

Arriving from other London airports
- London city: links to London via overground train or Docklands Light Railway. A taxi will cost around £20.

- Stansted: train to Liverpool Street station and National Express bus service. A taxi will cost about £35.

- Luton airport: a bus service to London. A taxi will cost about £50.

Main-line rail stations
London's main-line railway stations are:

- King's Cross/St Pancras (connecting northern England)
- Victoria (southern England)
- Liverpool Street (northern England)
- Paddington (west England)
- London Bridge (Kent and southeast England)
- Marylebone (west England and the Midlands)
- Charing Cross (southern England)

- Euston (northern England)

- Waterloo (southern England).

From these main-line stations the following additional transport systems are available:

1. Black taxi ranks, which are indicated. In addition Victoria station has a local taxi service which can prove to be cheaper than the black taxi.

2. Underground stations: although at St Pancras and Euston there is a short walk to the underground out of the main-line station. Follow the signs.

3. Local buses, with bus stops right outside the station.

Coaches
National Express coaches operate from Victoria coach station to all over the country. The coach station is not connected to the main-line train station or the underground; it is a walk of approximately 10 minutes. So, if you are arriving by coach keep in mind that carrying heavy bags and packages can prove difficult as you will need to cross a main road and navigate several steps.

However, travelling by coach is the cheapest way to travel in and out of London from most places in the UK. You may even consider that it is cheaper to take the coach to Victoria, then a taxi to your new home. There is a taxi rank close to the coach station.

By road
Travelling by road can be the most convenient way to transport your belongings, as you can take them right to your door. However, parking and unloading may be difficult. If you are using a removal company, the local council will allow loading and unloading to take place and even cordon off an area for you, providing they have been notified. Some councils make a charge for this service, some don't.

Most of central London has permit parking for residents only – which as a resident you will be grateful for. However, that means there are limited places to park and parking meters only allow parking for a maximum of four hours at a time. If you park illegally you will be towed away or clamped and it is very expensive and time-consuming to get your vehicle back.

A word of caution – when unloading your possessions always keep the vehicle locked or guarded.

CHECKLIST

1. Gather information on London districts from all sources and visit those areas you are interested in at different times of day and during different weather.

2. Work out a realistic timetable to move which fits your budget.

3. Plan your move and arrival in London with plenty of time.

3

Finding Accommodation

Once you have decided which area you would prefer to live in you will need to find suitable accommodation to fit your budget. There will always be some sort of accommodation available in London but much will depend on costs, preferences and your choice of area. An important tip is to put in energy and determination and stick at it. If you wish to buy a property it will not happen overnight so you may need to make temporary arrangements by renting or sharing.

RENTING PROPERTY

Long-term renting

Renting can be an excellent way to begin your life in London. It combines the best of both worlds, giving you a stable home, while allowing you to move on after the tenancy has been completed; usually six or twelve months. By then you should have a more definite idea of where you want to live, or indeed if you want to stay in the capital.

The majority of rented accommodation in London is fully-furnished. The availability of unfurnished accommodation is limited and can be even more expensive than furnished properties. In order to rent a property in London you will need:

- at least two months' rent in advance; one month as a deposit (sometimes six weeks' rent is required as a deposit)

- references or a credit search or both – you, as the potential tenant, will have to pay for the credit search

- proof that you are in regular employment or a guarantee from a parent or guardian if this is not yet the case

- the ability to sign a tenancy agreement for a minimum of six months, more likely twelve months

- deposits for any utilities (gas, electricity, etc) which may request them.

Short-term renting

If you want to rent a property short-term, i.e. less than six months, you will find the weekly rental fee much higher than with a long-term rental. Landlords consider that there is a higher risk of damage with short-term lets and the change-over is more frequent, leaving more chance for the property to stand empty and therefore be potentially less welcoming.

However, if you definitely only need somewhere for one or two months this is an option which could be investigated.

Points to note

You should always read any agreement through carefully before signing and if you are in any doubt about its meaning and validity always consult an expert. Note, however, that very few people use lawyers or other professionals when renting a property because tenancy agreements are so common in London and as a consequence are usually straightforward and simple. Consider the following:

1. Always take care when handing over any money, especially to individuals. Make sure that you obtain a receipt and proof that the funds are being held on your behalf as a deposit and/or rent.

2. Be prepared to take plenty of time to find the right accommodation for your requirements.

3. Keep a realistic view when visiting properties, in that you are not expecting too much for your budget.

4. Be aware that many properties in London do not look attractive from the outside and can have run down communal areas even though they are presentable inside.

5. Do not be pressurised into handing over money or signing an agreement until you are ready and happy with the situation.

6. You can always try to negotiate, even with rentals.

Rights and responsibilities of renting

There have been a large number of recent court cases concerning landlords and tenants and the law is constantly changing and being updated.

Many of the changes in law are to protect tenants and allow them to live more comfortably and free from hassle. However, a tenant has responsibilities towards the property and the landlord.

Responsibilities of tenants

1. To pay the rent in full and on time.

2. To pay the appropriate amount of council tax.

3. To pay for a television licence as needed.

4. To keep the property clean and tidy.

5. To carry out minor repairs, e.g. replacing light bulbs, fuses, etc.

6. To keep within the guidelines of the lease, e.g. not operating a business from the address, limiting noise, no sub-letting, etc.

7. To return the property to the landlord in a clean and tidy state.

Responsibilities of landlords

1. To ensure all major repairs are carried out.

2. To ensure all appliances are kept in working order.

3. To fulfil all safety requirements relating to gas and electrical appliances.

4. To keep neighbours from causing a disturbance as far as possible.

5. To respect the privacy of tenants.

6. To hand the property to the tenant in a clean and tidy state.

7. To pay the water rates.

The whole process from finding rented accommodation to moving in can take as little as one week; the normal timescale is 2–4 weeks (see Figure 1).

BUYING PROPERTY

The principles of buying a property in London are the same as buying a property anywhere else in England. It is always advisable to seek expert assistance. There are three main aspects which can hold up the purchase:

- how long it takes you to find a buyer for your present home

- how long it takes you to find a suitable property and have the offer accepted

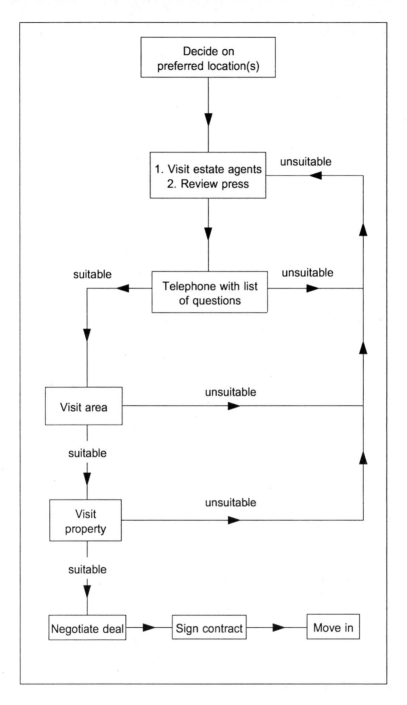

Fig. 1. Flowchart of renting property.

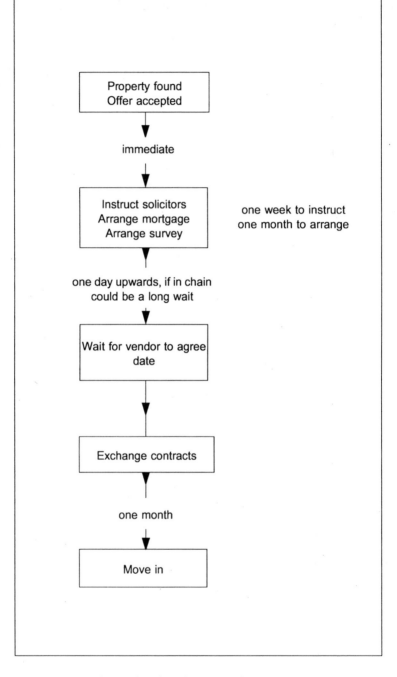

Fig. 2. Time flowchart to buying property.

- how long it takes for the current occupants to move out and the new occupants to move in to your present home.

(See Figure 2.)

Additional considerations when buying property in London
There are, however, additional concerns when buying any property in the capital.

1. The majority of properties are leasehold and the structure and time remaining on the lease will require additional attention.

2. Many properties in London were built on London clay and as such have dubious foundations. In general this causes few problems when living there, but you may find that securing a mortgage on the property is difficult and obtaining subsidence insurance is sometimes impossible.

3. Take extra care when you are informed that an area is 'up and coming' by an estate agent as this is tantamount to saying it is currently not a pleasant place to live but could be in the future – if people continue to renovate the area. On the other hand you could get a real bargain.

4. Some leasehold properties will offer the freehold of the site in addition to the leasehold. This is usually as a package, with the owners of the neighbouring flats, by way of a limited company. Each property owner will be a director of the limited company which owns the freehold. Although this sounds as if it will make the property more saleable, you must remember that you are in business with the other owners. Any financial problems which they have can end up as yours.

5. You will be responsible for service charges to maintain communal areas in flats. Check out these costs carefully by asking for, at least, the previous accounts back to when the communal areas, both inside and outside, were last redecorated. You may be surprised!

SHARING PROPERTY

Flat- or house-sharing is a popular, attractive alternative to renting a property on your own or buying in London. The vast majority of young people start their lives in London this way. It has several major advantages.

Advantages

- there is the opportunity to live in an area which you feel is more respectable or closer to your work

- the accommodation which you can afford is likely to be bigger and probably nicer

- it is much cheaper with regard to utility costs and rent

- you will always have company and friends to go out with

- it is a good way to get references for the future

- you can live with like-minded people.

Disadvantages

Great care needs to be taken when agreeing a sub-let of a room. You need to ensure that whoever the rent is being paid to is authorised to let the room to you. You need to see a copy of the original tenancy agreement. If sub-letting is not allowed you could find yourself not only homeless but losing some or all of your personal possessions. Always insist on a receipt for rent and deposits even if the agreement is verbal.

There are other disadvantages you should also be aware of.

- you may find that you have no time to yourself with a houseful of people all the time

- unless you are all like-minded you will need to draw up a rota for cleaning and tidying

- great care needs to be exercised relating to the use of utilities such as the telephone

- you can lose your home if one or more of the other tenants break the terms of the tenancy, unless each tenant has a separate agreement with the landlord

- if you find yourself living with the landlord if could prove uncomfortable if you have a problem relating to the tenancy

- you could find it chaotic.

Despite the numerous and often quite frightening disadvantages, house-sharing is the most popular method of living in London and often proves a great success. Many people thrive on this lifestyle and build up life-long friendships in the process.

APPROACHING AGENCIES

Estate agents are numerous in London. The advice they offer varies tremendously and whether you are renting, buying or sharing there will be an agency to help you. It pays to shop around and build up strong relationships with individuals in the agency as this will give you an advantage.

Although it is the vendor or the landlord who pays most of the fees to estate agents there are many agents in London who charge a 'registration fee' for putting you on their books as a prospective tenant.

Remember that all estate agents receive a high proportion of their salaries in commission. This means that they will be eager for you to buy or rent a property through them.

Some suggested questions to ask are:

1. Which areas does the company represent?

2. Which areas does the company have expertise in?

3. How long has the company been in existence? (Remember that the agency could be the ones holding your deposit, so if they are financially unstable you could lose it.)

4. How long have you, as an individual, been in the business?

REVIEWING APPROPRIATE PUBLICATIONS

As well as approaching an estate agent you will find many rental and shared properties are advertised in the local press. The main places to look are:

- the weekly local newspapers for the relevant areas of interest, which can be obtained by visiting local newsagents; free or for a small cost

- *Loot*; which is available every Thursday and is free for those who advertise in it

- the *Evening Standard*; which is available every afternoon and evening from Monday to Friday inclusive, although Wednesday, Thursday and Friday are the most relevant days.

The early bird...

It is imperative that you move quickly when the publication appears. This is especially true with rentals and sharing. Buy the papers early and telephone immediately. Arrange to see the properties as soon as possible and make your offer quickly if you are interested.

Although this may sound impossible to begin with, especially when you don't know the areas around London and have nothing to compare the properties with, you will soon find that you know exactly what you are looking for. Have patience.

Rental advertisements

These are typical examples of advertisements from the press relating to properties available for rent. There will be little information and it will be up to you to telephone to find out what you need to know before setting off to view. After a while you will learn to 'read between the lines', as well as to understand the bewildering array of abbreviations.

> **BARBICAN EC2** – Quality studio 5th floor £180 p.w. Tel: 0171...

> **BRIXTON** 1 bed flat, high standard, CH, 2 mins tube £180 p.w. Tel...

These adverts say very little about the flats and you will need to write down a list of questions to ask before telephoning. Although both of these properties are the same cost per week there are a number of additional factors which need to be taken into account.

Possible differences
- The council tax rate will differ as they are in different districts.

- How convenient are either of them to where you will be working or studying?

- What are the security aspects?

- One is in a large purpose-built block and one may well be in a terraced house. Which is which?

- Are they both the same size?

Can you spot any other factors which concern you or about which you would want more information?

W9 Excellent 1st fl 2 bed flat within 5 mins tube & bus. Bath with shw. Fully ft kit & lge lounge. Digital TV. £350 p.w. Tel:...	**NW3** – 3bd top fl flat. Female n/s to share. Own room. £100 p.w. inc. bills (not phone).

The advertisement on the left has slightly more detail, although you may wish to ask similar questions. However, you will need to find out where W9 is. Many advertisers use the London postal codes instead of area names and you will soon become accustomed to understanding their approximate location.

The advertisement on the right is for someone to share. It tells you that a female, non-smoker is sought to share a three bedroom flat in NW3. Rent and all bills, with the exception of the telephone, are £100 per week. What other questions would you ask?

Checklist of questions when telephoning about advertisements

1. Council tax area and band?
2. Which floor? Is there a garden?
3. Which is the closest and how far is the nearest tube station, bus stop and other transport?
4. What are the neighbours like?
5. What are the local facilities?
6. What is the state of decoration?
7. How long is the tenancy?
8. If sharing, who else shares? What do they do? How old are they?
9. Exact address and telephone number?

VISITING AREAS

You will already have chosen one or more areas where you believe you would like to live and may well have looked around them so when you get to the point of making a decision you should feel comfortable with your choice. On the other hand, you may feel that it needs further investigation. If you are likely to be living in the area for a while there are certain important ways to visit.

Always visit the property at night as well as during the day, and perhaps on a rainy day, so you can see it at its worst. Travel by tube or bus, get off at the closest station and walk the distance to the property. It will clarify the time taken from the nearest transport and give you a clear idea of how safe it will be. You are going to have to do this journey regularly when you move in, so check it out.

On the return journey travel back by a different method of transport. London Underground occasionally breaks down so you need to asses a variety of options of travelling around.

Local amenities

Visiting the area at the weekend can also give an insight into the local facilities around the area and how busy the area is. You may find shopping will be a problem because it is a long walk or bus journey to a supermarket. You may find that there is a local football pitch close by so that most Saturday afternoons are full of people and noise – which of course you may want! All of these aspects need to be considered.

LOOKING AROUND PREMISES

You will need to visit the actual properties to determine your interest. This can be difficult and embarrassing when you start out. Try not to get flustered and rush it. This is an important decision for you and there will be nothing worse than making an error which could last a good few months or even longer if you are buying. Be prepared for the fact that moving is expensive, time-consuming and unsettling.

If you realise immediately that you are not interested in the property it is always more sensible to let this be known. Do not waste anyone's time. Most people in London have little enough time anyway. You can do it kindly.

Ask yourself the following two questions: Can I see myself living here for six/twelve months? Do I want to live here for the next few years?

Points to remember
- be on time for appointments
- always appear friendly

- have a list of questions and ask them
- dress smartly
- be prepared to give a brief history about yourself.

All these pointers will show you as professional – a good prospective tenant.

SIGNING AGREEMENTS

When the point comes to signing the documentation, take your time. Read everything carefully before signing.

If you are in any doubt about any aspect of the documentation seek professional advice. Although it may cost extra money initially, it could save a lot of money and heartache in the longer term.

ORGANISING UTILITIES

If you are buying a property and have arranged your move through an agency they may well contact the appropriate utility companies for you. However, it is wise to contact utility companies yourself to ensure there will be no problems and that you understand the situation. The following is a guideline to assist you, although many utility companies now offer both gas and electricity supplies so you will need to check this aspect carefully.

British Gas

The home movers team needs to be notified at least 48 hours in advance of any move. The number is 0645 555 908, charged at a national rate. You may find that if you have not used gas facilities in your own name a deposit will be needed and/or a credit check made. You will receive advice on the different methods of payment available to you. British Gas now also offers electricity.

When you arrive at your new accommodation you will need to telephone 0645 555 909 with the meter reading. This is much easier than asking someone to call to read the meter.

London Electricity

There is a freephone number available to give the 48 hours' notice required – 0800 096 9000. You may find that a credit reference and/ or deposit is required and you can arrange a time for the meter to be read within a two-hour span on the day you move in, or you can read it yourself. London Electricity now also offers gas.

You will be given a reference number and details of the direct debit scheme which saves money on the quarterly charge.

British Telecom

If you wish to take over an existing telephone line you need to give 48 hours' notice by dialling 150, which is free. You will find this number useful, along with your local telephone directory.

British Telecom offers a wide range of services to its customers and has tried to improve the service offered by training its employees in all manner of ways. You may therefore find that they will attempt to sell you a massive range of products when you call. Be aware of the costs!

If you need a new telephone line installed you will need to give a longer notice period and it will cost more. This will vary according to the area so it is prudent to notify BT as soon as possible.

Water supply

The water supply will not be disconnected and you will be able to advise the appropriate company of the change of name when you move in. See your local telephone directory.

Council tax

You will be able to notify the local council when you move in. You will be sent a bill almost immediately and you should be aware that if you are living on your own you are allowed a 25 per cent discount on the bill. You should claim this before paying as it will not be automatically deducted.

Other organisations to notify

When moving to London you should be aware of the following:

- your car insurance may increase

- you can arrange for the post office to forward your mail from your previous address

- household contents insurance will increase, especially if you are in a ground-floor flat without window bars.

If you are sharing you will not need to notify the utilities, although it would seem sensible to have at least one utility in your name as proof of residence. In London, proof of identify is often requested by a utility bill in your name as well as a driver's licence. (Beware, however, that in a flat-share you could get into trouble if the utility in your name is not paid by any other members of the house – you will be liable for their share.)

CHECKLIST

1. Visit all the estate agents in the areas with a list of criteria.

2. Buy the relevant publications as and when they are available.

3. Continue to visit the areas you are most interested in.

4. Keep notes of addresses and telephone numbers to hand as you may have to move quickly.

5. Make a list of everyone who needs to be notified of a change of address.

6. Keep positive and don't settle for second-best.

4

Living in London

There are several aspects which need to be taken into account when you finally move into your new residence and start to live in London. At first you may feel that it is all a dream and will be delighted just to be there. However, the stresses and strains of any move can weigh heavily on anyone, so take your time and adjust to your new home-town gradually. There are several factors you need to take into account.

ACCLIMATISING TO THE PACE

You will know when you have fully adjusted to the pace in London; you will be walking at the same pace as everyone else around you! When you return to your home town or city you will find yourself walking faster than everyone else. It is not just about walking pace though. Pace also refers to a way of life, habits and general attitudes.

- Attitudes when driving around. Although the speed you can actually drive around London may be slower than you are accustomed to, because of the quantity of traffic, the speed cars move in and out of junctions is probably faster. You will be hooted at if you sit at a green traffic light for more than a split second.

- Adroitness when paying for goods in a queue. Everyone will always have their money or credit card at the ready. Time is precious.

- When crossing the road, as a pedestrian, you need to take care. It can be hazardous as many cars do not stop at zebra crossings in London. Always move with speed and wave your thanks if they do stop. Until you are accustomed to the traffic, the one-way streets and general attitudes on the road, always cross at appropriate road crossings and keep alert.

How long will it take to adjust?

Adjustment time will vary from person to person. It may be that you will fall into the quick pace easily. You may feel little difference until you leave the capital, when you may find yourself feeling exhausted once you slow down. On the other hand, you may find yourself exhausted from day one. If it's the latter then be kind to yourself and get plenty of rest. You will adjust.

TRAVELLING AROUND

By underground

London Underground covers the tube network. The underground, or tube, as it is known, is one of the most efficient ways to travel around the capital. It can, however, be amazingly misleading in terms of understanding where one place is in relation to another.

The map of the underground on display has been specially designed to make travelling around it simple and clear. The actual tube lines do not run as indicated except in relation to each other. You will be able to see this clearly when you refer to a street map.

For example: this means that you can get on the underground to go from Leicester Square to Covent Garden to find that it would have been much quicker to walk the few hundred yards along Long Acre. Here are some pointers to make travelling on the underground easier:

- the underground operates Monday to Sunday, 364 days a year (not Christmas Day), from approximately 05.50 to 24.30 – shorter hours on Sundays

- the system is shown on maps by coloured lines which are easy to follow – each colour represents a different line

- check which line you need, which direction – north, south, east or west – and the name of the stop at the end of the line you will be travelling on, as this will appear on the front of the train and also on the indicator on the platform

- the indicators on the platforms will show the final destination of the train as it approaches as well as how many minutes before the anticipated time of arrival of the train

- when changing tube lines follow the signs which indicate directions, e.g. 'Circle Line – eastbound via King's Cross'

- when arranging to meet people always ask them which tube station is the closest

- consult the London Underground tube map if travelling at weekends, some stations are not open on Saturdays and/or Sundays.

Types of ticket
You will be able to obtain a free leaflet at your local tube station which covers underground and bus fares within Greater London.

There are a variety of tickets which can reduce the cost of travel. The longer the period of ticket purchased the cheaper each individual journey will work out. Try to get to grips with the London underground zone system – this can assist with any journey. Zone 1 is the centre of the City, the area of the Circle line and inside it. Zone numbers go outwards to Zone 6 which is on the outskirts of London as far as Heathrow.

Note the following:

- stations at the northern end of the Metropolitan line are outside Greater London and subject to different fares, which are listed at the relevant stations

- if you are travelling on the Bakerloo line north of Queen's Park the fare rate is different, but full details are on display at the appropriate stations.

The main types of tickets are detailed below. Many are available at local newsagents as well as underground stations, London Transport travel information centres and some national railway stations.

1. You can purchase a **single ticket** for each journey separately as you travel. This can prove to be expensive if you travel frequently, although definitely the best bet for the occasional journey.

2. You can buy a **return ticket** which is exactly the same price as two single tickets to and from your destination. The only advantage to this type of ticket is that you will not have to queue twice.

3. You can purchase a **one-day Travelcard** if you begin your journey after 09.30. You can complete your journey at any time within

the day the ticket is dated and use the ticket as often as you like within the stated zone(s) and date. This is excellent value if you are travelling frequently on one day.

4. **Weekend Travelcards** are similar to the one-day Travelcard, but allow you to travel on the two weekend 'days and/or two consecutive days during public holidays.

5. **Seven-day Travelcards** within specified zones allow as many journeys as you wish within the days and zones. This is a great value ticket for commuters, especially if you are paid weekly.

6. **One-month Travelcards** within specified zones allow you to travel as often as you wish within the zones stated on the ticket for one month. Take care if you are taking an annual holiday when purchasing such a ticket. The saving is excellent for frequent travellers. Note that most people seem to purchase these types of ticket on the first day of each month, so there can be long queues. They are available from any start date in the month.

7. **Three-month Travelcards** can be purchased and London Transport will always be willing to price a ticket for a different period. These types of ticket are the least regularly purchased.

8. **Annual Travelcards** are usually bought by employees of companies which give an interest-free season ticket loan as one of the benefits. It is a great benefit. Your saving will be huge and you only have the hassle once a year of purchasing a ticket. However, you need to make sure you will not be cashing it in. The 'cash-in price' is calculated to allow for the fact that you would have been travelling for the expired period of time. Briefly, if you cash-in a one-year ticket after six months you will not receive as much as half of the money back; you will receive the sum paid originally less the cost of a six-month ticket. This is to stop people buying annual tickets then cashing them in straight away. You can also purchase an **annual 'gold card' season ticket** for an additional sum which gives you extra entitlements.

9. **Carnet tickets** are available in books of ten tickets. These can be bought in advance for travel within Zone 1 only. They represent a large saving on the purchase on ten standard single tickets within the zone.

10. **Family Travelcards** and **group day tickets** (for groups over ten) are also available.

11. **Discounts** are available for children and teenagers up to 17 years old, and 18–24-year-olds participating in the 'New Deal' programme can obtain a leaflet from the Employment Services which will allow discounts.

In order to purchase a Travelcard of seven days or more you will need to get a photocard which has to be kept with the ticket at all times. These are available with:

● passport photograph and resident details

● a completed application form – available at your local underground station.

Excess fares
If you travel beyond your Travelcard zone without paying the additional fare or have the wrong ticket or no ticket at all for your journey you will be subject to a Penalty Fare which is demanded on the spot. If you are in any doubt about which ticket to purchase always ask an official.

By bus
The bus system is more complicated than the underground system and requires careful studying. There are free bus maps available which will assist you. Different areas have different named bus systems, so it is essential to acquire the relevant bus map(s) for your area. You need to be aware that there are no tie-ins between the train, underground and bus systems in London.

Although the bus network is usually slower than the tube, it is an excellent way to get to see the sights and where each place is in relation to the other. Many tourists pay to go on London sightseeing tours. It can also be more pleasant and safer, particularly late at night. Night-buses operate throughout the night and the bus number is prefixed with 'N'.

Many London Underground Travelcards can be used on the stated zones on the bus network and night-bus services. Check locally for confirmation.

By train
Since privatisation the railway network around London has become much more complicated. Different networks go into each mainline station. It is possible to buy combined tickets between the

underground and mainline train networks. The best advice is to investigate at your local station.

By taxi

Travelling around London by taxi is expensive. There are numerous taxi companies operating throughout London. The majority are licensed and fair, however, do be careful as there are always one or two 'taxi' companies which have no licence and no insurance.

Black cabs are known throughout the world and are often seen as the most knowledgeable and honest of all taxi drivers. In order to obtain a licence for a black taxi the driver must pass an examination known as 'The Knowledge'. It is a test on all streets throughout central London. Important points to know about black cabs:

- they are available 365 days and nights of the year, although there is an additional surcharge on Sundays, Bank Holidays and late at night, which can double the price of the journey

- they only have to take you within a radius of six miles from the centre of London, although you may be able to negotiate a longer journey, especially to an airport

- in theory, they cannot refuse to take you to your destination if it is within the six-mile radius of the centre, if you are sensible, and the yellow light is on indicating availability

- each taxi has a licence plate inside and outside the taxi so if you have any complaints you know who to complain about.

Advantages of black taxis compared to ordinary taxi companies
- the driver is more likely to know how to get to your exact destination, without assistance, by the quickest or shortest route

- the prices are fixed by the distance and/or the time of the journey and the meter is clearly visible at all times

- each taxi is registered and licensed

- taxis can be stopped in the street when the yellow light on the top of the cab is on

- you do not have to ask for a price when you get in, the meter shows your charge as your journey progresses.

Disadvantages of black taxis compared to ordinary taxi companies
- black taxis are usually more expensive – they can be up to twice the price for long distances, for example to airports

- if there is congestion a black taxi may be sitting with the meter continuing to run whereas an ordinary taxi will have quoted you a fixed fee for the journey in advance (always ensure you have arranged this before getting into the taxi)

- ordinary taxis can be much more readily available for long distances

- ordinary taxis cannot be stopped in the street – legally.

By car

Driving in London requires special skills. Of primary importance is patience. You will not be driving anywhere with speed. The average car speed in central London is 10 miles per hour – if you are lucky. You will find that drivers pull in and out of junctions quicker and with fewer gaps between cars than you might be used to. Always allow twice as long as you think it will take when you decide to drive anywhere. Within a few weeks it will become second nature. You also need to become aware of the many one-way streets in London which can end up sending you round in circles, or to a dead end. Nicholson's *Streetfinder* has all London's one-way streets.

If you think driving is difficult, wait until you try to park. Central London is full of residents' parking areas (for residents only), parking meters (fixed charge), single yellow lines (no parking between 08.30 and 18.30 Mon–Fri, 08.30–13.30 Sat, but permitted on Sunday), double yellow lines (no parking at any time) and double red lines. You do not need to learn what all these mean except for the fact that there is no free parking!

The resident's parking permit system works on an alphabetical basis. For those living in the permit area it has provided at least a vague possibility of being able to park somewhere near where you live. A parking permit does not guarantee you a place to park. It merely allows you to park in the appointed alphabetical zone, should there be a space.

If you have always found parking in tight spaces difficult then take some time out to practise. It has become an essential art in London.

In order to qualify for a parking permit you have to prove the following:

- You live at the qualifying address. You have to prove you stay overnight for at least three nights each week. This can be done by the electoral register or a letter of confirmation from the estate agents.

- You own the vehicle in question or have a right to drive it. This can be done by the vehicle registration document or a note from the owner listed on the document; for example, if it is a company car.

There is a fee to be paid for the permit, which varies from area to area, and you will receive a permit which must be displayed close to the tax disc at all times. Placing a notice stating that you have applied for a permit will not stop your car being clamped or towed away. Each council district will have an office which you can visit to acquire the permit. This is well worth doing as it may take seven days or more by post. The costs and time to retrieve a car from the pound or get it unclamped are huge.

By bicycle

Many younger people choose to cycle around London and in a test carried out a few years ago, when there was a full public transport strike, a bicycle proved to be the fastest way to get around. It was even quicker than a motorbike because it could get through smaller gaps.

Although there are still relatively few cycle lanes in London, it has proved to be a convenient, cheap, healthy and trendy way to travel around. Some companies are beginning to offer financial incentives to encourage employees to cycle to work. The following are points to be aware of:

- always lock (preferably an iron-bar one) your cycle to an immovable object when leaving it

- ensure there are security markings on your cycle

- organise a sensible place to keep the cycle where you live – preferably locked inside – you may need special permission for this

- always wear a crash helmet and safety pads when cycling around the centre of London

- consider wearing a breathing mask, particularly in the centre

- take great care as many buses and taxis believe the roads belong to them
- make sure your cycle is insured.

By motorcycle
A quick and convenient method to travel around. Take similar precautions to cycling. Many streets have designated areas to park for motorcycles without the need for parking permits.

On foot
If you go to New York many people walk to and from work, in training shoes, to get regular exercise. This is not so in London. However, it is a cheap and easy way to get around. It can be as quick (or quicker) as any bus, especially in rush hour. There are some shorter journeys where it is easier, quicker and less distance to walk than using the tube.

AVOIDING STRESS

There are a multitude of pressures and strains on anyone living in London. These include:

- long working hours
- a fast pace
- long commuting times
- impatience of others
- a need to stay streetwise.

A brief mention has already been made about combating stress, but it is important to understand when you are suffering from it. It affects different people in different ways, so there is no definitive answer to the problem. As mentioned in Chapter 2, there are three main stages:

Stage 1. Alarm – initial panic in a new situation. This is usually short-lived.

Stage 2. Resistance – where you feel you have the ability to continue despite the new situation. This allows you to keep fighting a particular cause of stress and lasts longer than Stage 1.

Stage 3. Exhaustion. This happens after you have been in the situation for some time. It can also occur after you have moved in and started work. It may show itself by an illness, such as a virus or cold.

All three stages eventually produce the effect of adrenal exhaustion. This is brought about by overworked adrenal glands having an effect on the regulation of the hormone levels. Signs of being stressed are:

- difficulties with your digestion
- difficulties with your nervous system
- deterioration of the condition of your skin, hair and nails
- speeding up of your heart-rate.

If you believe you may be suffering from stress, the following ways are recognised as helping to alleviate it:

- avoid stimulants including tea, coffee, alcohol and cigarettes
- eat raw fruit, vegetables and keep to a healthy diet
- learn to meditate or relax
- take regular exercise
- avoid stress for at least one day each week.

If in doubt seek medical advice

BECOMING STREETWISE

Being streetwise can be defined as 'familar with the ways of modern urban life'. This definition needs to have more added to it. It hardly expresses the importance, to anyone living and travelling around a large city on their own, of being alert and sensible. It is essentially about using your common sense. Here are some do's and don'ts:

Do:
- wear comfortable shoes which allow you to move quickly should you need to

- carry spare cash and identification in a separate pocket in case your main wallet or handbag is stolen

- keep your house and car keys out of your main bag or pocket

- keep your cheque book and cheque card in different pockets or bags
- tell a friend or family member of your plans and let them know if they change, as someone should know your whereabouts at all times
- take a black taxi if it is late at night
- ask directions from the police, transport officials or shopkeepers – not individuals in the street
- arrange to meet friends in indoor locations.

Don't:
- get in a tube or railway carriage on your own, find one with other people in
- wear high-heeled shoes; these reduce your mobility
- approach any stranger in the street to ask directions
- stop to answer questions in the street, no matter how innocent the questioner appears
- stand studying a map in the street and make it obvious you are lost
- stand on street corners waiting to meet people.

KEEPING PERSPECTIVE

It can sometimes be difficult to keep perspective when you hear that:

- you need to be streetwise
- you shouldn't talk to strangers
- people will cheat you
- and all manner of other evil deeds.

This is not the only side to the equation. London offers a huge amount of opportunity, fun and friendships for everyone. It is sometimes talked about as being a lonely place, which can be true, but you can also develop the deepest and truest friendships ever.

Opportunities
Many people come to London to find fame and fortune. It is not

guaranteed. You will still need to work hard and prove yourself. However, in virtually every walk of life there are more opportunities in London than most other places.

Many Londoners are happy to go about their business without the thought of fame and fortune. They enjoy the buzz and pace of life.

Fun

Opportunities for fun and excitement are immense. Wherever you go something is always happening. You can eat whatever type of food you want and go to whatever type of entertainment you want.

Many young people find the clubbing scene to be the most exciting they have ever come across.

CHECKLIST

1. Obtain a map of the underground and local bus map with details of ticket prices.

2. Learn how the public transport systems work in your area.

3. Investigate the parking situation and any necessary permits needed for your area.

4. Keep fit and healthy and organise rest time.

5. Keep a healthy perspective.

5

Applying for a Job

The process of searching for a job can be both daunting and exciting – at the same time. It can provide an opportunity to change direction and/or be the beginning of a whole new life and career.

There has been a definite change from the 'jobs for life' idea over the last 10 to 15 years. Most people will change jobs, if not careers, at least a few times during their working life. This is especially true somewhere as fast-moving as London.

Definition of job-hunting
You will need to be clear in your own mind as to your aims as well as dedicated to the process of job search for it to be successful. Job searching is a full-time job in itself.

COMPOSING A CV

Once you have decided on your target career(s) you will need to produce a CV (or curriculum vitae). This is a self-marketing document which has the sole purpose of gaining you an interview. Remember that a CV will not get you a job; that is not its function. That is the purpose of the interview. A CV needs to be constructed in such a way that whoever reads it will want to interview you – they will want to know more about you. If you are searching for jobs or careers in more than one area you will need more than one CV.

Research indicates that most recruitment personnel will spend between 30 and 180 seconds reading a CV – with the vast majority around 60 seconds. You need to keep that fact in mind when you are creating it – it is vital to get across the important points concisely and clearly.

Assembling the facts
The start point is to assemble all the facts you will need for the CV:

- name, address, contact telephone numbers, e-mail address, etc.

- personal details, including your date of birth, marital status, interests, etc.

- education details with dates and examination grades achieved

- previous work experience, including all part-time and Saturday work, with dates

- any additional information which would show a level of responsibility, commitment and discipline, such as captain of a sports' team, completing a marathon, etc.

- any useful, additional knowledge such as computer skills, presentation skills, etc.

Considering an appropriate layout
Choosing a CV format for today's job market can be perplexing. There are hundreds of books on the market, all with differing ideas of the 'correct' format. Details of suggested further reading are given at the end of this book. There is no such thing as a perfect format, but a few points should be kept in mind for clarity of information:

- keep the wording simple, positive and objective, and back it up with facts

- be honest, as details will be checked

- keep the format clear and plain, making it easy to read the salient points

- keep to one page, if possible, and certainly no more than two pages.

Dos, don'ts and maybes

Do:
- use good quality, white paper of at least 80g

- post all applications first class; if faxed always post a copy as well

- get the CV professionally printed

- keep the CV up to date

- ensure that the CV is correctly spelt and laid out

- hand-write an accompanying letter.

NAME
Address
telephone number, fax number, e-mail

WORK EXPERIENCE (in reverse chronological order – keep relevant to job you're applying for)

ORGANISATION
A short statement describing the function, service or products.

Job Title   **Dates**
A short statement describing your function within the organisation.

- highlight your achievements, strengths, profitability
- responsibilities are important but are not, in themselves, success indicators
- where possible, show the scope of your achievements by quantifying and/or qualifying them
- keep specific and do not waffle.

ORGANISATION
Job Title   **Dates**
- repeat the above format
- the further back you go, the less space should be needed
- do not leave any gaps in your dates.

EDUCATION & QUALIFICATIONS
List in reverse chronological order
Name of university/college/school with dates
Itemise 'A' and 'O' levels, GCSE, further education subjects, degree, etc.

TRAINING
Highlight relevant training courses together with dates.

INTERESTS
No more than four, no less than two. Include anything and everything!

PERSONAL DETAILS
Date of birth (month as a word)
Marital status

Fig. 3. Example of a CV.

Do not:

- attach photographs, written references etc. unless specifically requested in the advertisement

- be dishonest about qualifications and work experience as many companies use 'CV detectives' these days to check the accuracy of all of these facts

- send old photocopies with dirty marks or black lines marked on

- hand-write a CV

- e-mail details without a follow-up telephone call.

Maybe:

- use cream-coloured paper (this can be considered acceptable)

- include a brief summary or profile of yourself at the top of the CV

- send it by e-mail, although ensure contact details are clear and follow up to be certain that it has been received.

APPLYING IN WRITING

Composing a letter

A letter of application needs to be carefully planned. This could be all that stands between you and the next candidate in the allotted '60 seconds'. The letter of application should be kept positive and accurate.

Never start a letter with a negative statement such as, 'Although I do not have the relevant qualifications I feel I would be an asset to your company because...'. Your CV will probably never even be read.

For any job in today's market there will be hundreds of applications. The person whose task it is to read all the CVs will be only too pleased to have one fewer to read. You need to take the same care with the covering letter as with the CV itself. Here are two examples of covering letters. Judge for yourself which you believe will be the most effective.

Clearly the second letter has assisted the reader by giving details of relevant experience and knowledge. It helps the reader pick out the salient points on the CV. He or she can scan the CV, saving valuable time and seeing immediately which aspects are relevant.

```
                                              Simon Smith
                                                 Flat 100
                                                The Road
                                                  London
                                         Telephone number
                                                     Date

Dear Mr Falley

I have enclosed my CV for the job of Office Manager. As you will see I
have relevant experience

Yours sincerely


Simon Smith
```

Fig. 4. Example of covering letter: 1.

```
                                              Simon Smith
                                                 Flat 100
                                                The Road
                                                  London
                                         Telephone number
                                                     Date

Dear Mr Falley

                        Office Manager

I have enclosed my CV for the position of Office Manager as
advertised in the local paper today. As you will see from my CV I have
the following experience which I believe fits in well with your
specification:

•  previous managerial experience of teams of up to ten people
•  knowledge of employment law
•  expertise in the industry sector

I look forward to hearing from you in due course, but in the meantime
if you need any additional information please feel free to contact me
on the above quoted number.

Yours sincerely


Simon Smith
```

Fig. 5. Example of a covering letter: 2.

Completing an application form

More and more organisations are using application forms. They can be difficult and cumbersome to complete. For an organisation they have the following advantages:

1. All information provided to the company is in the same format and order so comparisons between applicants are easier to make.

2. A company can ask for exactly the type and amount of information it needs to make a decision to interview.

3. Many companies are trying to offer equal opportunities to all applicants and this type of format offers less chance of any bias.

4. A completed application form has to be signed and will form part of the contract of employment. This means any dishonest claims on the form can allow the company to dismiss the applicant.

Despite the numerous good reasons for application forms most people dislike filling them in. Here are some useful pointers to making it a more successful event:

1. Always take a photocopy of the form before starting to fill it in. Complete the photocopy in pencil and transfer your wording to the original copy when you are fully satisfied with the pencilled-in document.

2. Please follow the instructions. If it states: 'Fill this application form in with black pen', then fill it in with black pen, otherwise it is unlikely to be read or at least you will have annoyed the reader before you even start.

3. When there is a large space headed: 'Additional information' or 'Detail any other aspects which may help with the decision', then fill the box with positive background information. Do not leave it blank. This is your opportunity to show individuality.

4. Be honest.

5. Take as much time completing the form as you would writing a CV. This will put you at an advantage over the vast majority of applicants, many of whom do not take enough care with application forms.

6. It is acceptable to send your CV in with the application form but never leave a gap on the application form and write, 'See CV'. It indicates laziness.

RESPONDING TO THE OPEN JOB MARKET

The open job market consists of those jobs which are being advertised and sought openly by recruitment agencies and organisations.

It is generally believed that only 40 per cent of all jobs are advertised openly. The other 60 per cent are known as the hidden job market, see page 62.

Replying to advertisements

Care needs to be taken when responding to any advertisement. Always read it through carefully before beginning to compose your letter.

Exercise

Assess the job advertisement below by the following:

- what age group are they looking for?
- which qualifications are they looking for?
- what salary is being offered?
- why is the application being processed in this manner?
- what experience is necessary?
- general layout and wording.

JMM RECRUITMENT GROUP
Magical Reception
London £18,000 plus great benefits

We have three exciting positions for three dynamic professionals. We are looking for fun-loving, interesting individuals who want to work in a creative industry sector. Jobs are in the City, West End and Battersea. If you have a proven track record as a receptionist and are seeking a role providing excellent perks call now for an immediate interview.

Telephone…at JMM Recruitment Group on…

Reviewing the advertisement

The wording is clear and simple and requests a telephone call to a recruitment company. The recruitment company will either ask for a CV to be sent or, if you are persuasive enough, an interview will be arranged where you will have to produce a CV. This is a common way of advertising and may be used as a filter. Using this method the recruitment company will not receive masses of CVs unless they are interested in the individuals.

Age and educational background are not specified, hinting at the fact that these will be secondary to any previous experience as a receptionist.

The salary details are specific, although there are clearly benefits (which need to be fully understood) in addition to the base salary.

Before telephoning you will need to prepare yourself. It is effectively a telephone interview. See 'direct approaches by telephone', later in this chapter.

Defining a recruitment agency

There can be confusion about the differences between various recruitment agencies. This guide should help:

1. Recruitment consultants or employment agencies are organisations which try to match job vacancies with suitable applicants. They will keep both vacancies and CVs of individuals on file. They can be involved with jobs at any level of salary although it is usually at the lower end of the salary scale.

2. Executive search consultants suggest that they do not keep CVs on file. Some do. They take job vacancies and search for suitable applicants, either through advertising or asking around the job market. These positions are usually at the middle to higher end of the salary scale.

3. Headhunters consider themselves to be the elite in job searching. They operate in a similar manner to executive search consultants, but they do not advertise positions. Salaries are usually at the highest level.

Signing on at recruitment agencies

Any recruitment agency has, by law, to make a check on the facts you declare on your CV. So, if you claim that you can type at 60 words per minute, you should be tested. There are hundreds of agencies, so it is impossible to sign on with all of them. Here are some pointers to making your choice:

1. Wherever possible go by personal recommendation.

2. Try to build up a relationship with one individual at the agency. Meet him or her and abide by their rules. If he or she says that they will call you, wait for the call. Do not hassle him or her. However, if you continually do not receive the call move on to another agency.

3. Insist you are informed each time your CV is sent to a company.

4. Do not sign on with masses of different agencies. If you do this you will not be able to keep track of your CV. As a consequence it could easily be sent to the same company by more than one agency, which is destructive.

APPROACHING THE HIDDEN JOB MARKET

Definition
The hidden job market refers to those jobs which have yet to be advertised in the press or referred to a recruitment agency. They are more difficult to find but if you do, your chances of success are increased as you will have a headstart on any competition. There are many reasons why an organisation has not arranged a recruitment campaign, such as:

- the previous employee has only just resigned
- the company is expanding rapidly and because of this has not yet defined the role
- they have just tried to recruit unsuccessfully and are taking another look at what type of individual is needed
- the company is unsure of the level of person needed.

There are two main ways to tap the hidden job market.

Networking
Networking is not about telephoning friends and asking for a job. It is about contacting people you know to ask for help. Here is an example of a typical networking conversation:

You: 'I've just moved to London and want to work in the hotel sector. I need some help. I don't have much information and I don't know anyone in the sector. I was wondering if you may be able to point me in the right direction.'

Your friend: 'I don't think so. I don't really have any knowledge about it. But my flatmate has a sister who used to be a receptionist in a hotel. I'll have a chat with him and see what he says.'

You may find that when your friend calls back his flatmate's sister will be quite willing to talk to you. She may have the name of a contact or two. Again, when you speak to her do not ask for a job, ask for help and advice.

As you continue with your networking you will be given more names. Carry on with the process and eventually you will talk to people within the sector(s) of your choice.

Direct approaches

Direct approaches can be made in three ways:

1. Letter.
2. Telephone contact.
3. Personal visit.

Think of your direct approach more as a business proposal than a job application. You will not be contacting the company in response to a particular job advertisement so you need to convince whoever you have contact with that you have something to offer him or her.

By letter

This is considered to be the easiest of the direct approach methods. A well-constructed letter should:

- to be addressed to a specific, relevant person

- ask for a meeting and not a job

- be well written, on quality stationery, specifying exactly where you can help and be as creative as possible

- be followed up by a telephone call.

By telephone

Any telephone call to a potential employer, networking contact or recruitment agency needs to be treated as a telephone interview. Here is a suggested technique:

1. Collect all pertinent information, including your CV, and settle in a room without noise or interruption.

2. Have paper and pen and list all the questions you wish to ask.

3. Prepare in rough any information you wish to get across.

4. Smile as you speak, it will sound more attractive.

5. Be persistent and arrange a time with the person or his or her secretary when he or she will be available to talk.

By personal visit

Personal visits are the most difficult of all the ways to approach companies direct. However, they show a level of determination which could put you ahead of other potential applicants. Here are some tips:

*   ensure you have a clean copy of your CV to leave

*   do not insist on seeing anyone as they may be busy, but try to make an appointment

*   be pleasant and confident

*   ask for a meeting to discuss opportunities

*   collect relevant leaflets and information which will assist you should you get an interview.

SUCCEEDING AT INTERVIEW

When you receive the letter, or more usually the telephone call, asking you for an interview you will undoubtedly be excited. The dictionary definition of an interview is 'an oral examination of an applicant for employment'. However, it should be viewed as a two-way process. You, the applicant, need to decide if the company is suitable for you. You may be lucky enough to have to choose between two or more companies, so you need to collect relevant information.

Preparing for the interview

The more time you spend on preparation the more comfortable you will feel about the interview. If you have got the interview through a recruitment agency they should be able to give you some hints and tips about what is expected of you. Useful considerations are:

1. Visit the premises before the interview, trying to arrive at the same time of day as your interview. This will help ensure you arrive on time. You do not need to enter the building, but take note of the type of clothes being worn by those going in and out of it.

2. Telephone the company and ask for any information leaflets on their products and services. You do not need to identify yourself, although if you tell the receptionist you will be attending an interview you could acquire an ally.

3. Follow the other methods of additional research which are detailed in Chapter 6.

Planning the structure of an interview

There will be questions you want to ask and information you want to know. How much will be dependent on a large number of factors; here are a few of the most important ones:

- salary level and benefits package
- working hours and conditions
- reporting structure
- promotion prospects.

The format for interviews will vary. Here is the most standard approach:

1. The interviewer will give a brief history of the company and detail the job position which is vacant. This could take about 10 to 15 minutes.

2. The interviewer will ask questions on aspects of your life – both professional and personal, using your CV as a basis. This may last around 30 minutes.

3. The interviewer will offer you an opportunity to ask any questions you may have. Try to come up with some.

4. The interview will be wound up with details of the next stage.

Answering questions

You will find as you attend more interviews that the same questions will come up. It is never a good idea to have your answers memorised perfectly, although some idea of what you are going to say is essential. Here are some common interview questions:

1. Tell me about yourself.

2. Why would you like this job?

3. What salary are you looking for?

4. If I were to ask your best friend what would he or she say was your main weakness?

5. What are your main strengths?

6. What did you most like/dislike about your previous job?

7. Where do you see yourself in five/ten years' time?

8. What are/were your reasons for leaving your current/previous job?

9. Why should I recruit you ahead of the other applicants?

10. Give me an example of something you are proud of.

Asking questions

An interviewer will always be impressed if you ask well-thought through questions. Make a note of all the information you wish to find out in advance and if it has not been covered by the end of the interview do not be afraid of asking.

KEEPING POSITIVE

Searching for a suitable job can become depressing as you are almost certain to receive some rejection letters along the way. It is important not to allow this to stop you from continuing your pursuit. Keeping positive is important. Here are some ways to achieve this:

1. Talk to friends and family about your efforts.

2. Keep healthy by eating well and taking regular exercise.

3. Learn to relax.

4. Keep several things going at once. If you are on a second or third interview keep applying for other jobs until you have the job offer, in writing, that you want.

CHECKLIST

1. Collect all the information relevant for your CV.

2. Produce a quality CV.

3. Approach the job search in a methodical manner.

4. Contact all your friends to let them know what you are looking for.

5. Keep a detailed notebook of all your endeavours.

6

Hunting for the Right Job

Seeking work in and around London demands a structured approach. By now you should be in the process of preparing your CV or already have it prepared. You will need to be focused and professional in every aspect of your job search. Once you have settled into your accommodation you have to get yourself organised with the following:

1. A work area with enough space and quiet to allow you to concentrate.

2. A system for answering telephone calls, with a method of sending and receiving faxes. This will include a telephone answering machine with a business-like message recorded. It will also mean a discussion between the other residents living in the accommodation, if there are any, about answering each telephone call in a professional manner during the period of the job search.

3. Access to a computer, preferably connected to the Internet, with a laser or ink-jet printer.

4. A supply of high-quality stationery.

5. A regular, daily routine which treats the process of job search as a full-time job. This will give you a sense of purpose each day as well as increase your chances of finding appropriate employment more quickly.

6. A diary and job search notebook to keep all relevant information.

ANALYSING OPPORTUNITIES

Within the methods of seeking employment mentioned in Chapter 5 you will need to consider the following:

- what type and level of role you are looking for
- what type and style of organisation you would prefer to work for
- which area of London you would prefer to work in, although this has been covered in detail in Chapter 2, it may be necessary to continually review possible work locations.

You will find the broadest variety of styles and roles possible in London so it is important to acknowledge the range of choice but not allow yourself to become undecided and unfocused because of it. If you prefer you can concentrate on more than one area at a time, however, you need to research each area carefully so a list of priorities is an essential start-point.

Deciding on your preferred type and level of role

If you are moving to London with a previous employment history then you need to decide what level of position you will be aiming for. It could be that you want to:

- keep to a similar position and role as previous jobs
- try to progress to the next stage in your career ladder
- change your role and/or sector completely.

Some points to bear in mind:

1. Companies in London tend to be larger than in rural areas and smaller cities. This leads to the job roles being more specialised, therefore, requiring a more in-depth knowledge.

2. As a generalisation many London companies consider themselves to be more professional than their provincial counterparts. This may or may not be true, but means that any prospective employee has to appear more professional in their approach.

3. Many London firms are the British, European or even worldwide headquarters of the organisation which means more responsibility and decision-making power. Any change or advancement which you may consider acceptable in a company outside London could prove difficult to achieve in these circumstances.

Your first job
If you are approaching the job search direct from an educational background, as a first job, your research into the organisations will be imperative. It can give you an insight into the appropriate level at which your exact qualifications will allow you to enter the company. Research will show you the style of organisation you are approaching to allow you to tailor your proposal accordingly.

Review the following advertisement and decide which level applies to you.

Large, well-known department store seeks all levels of first jobber. Do you want to work for this world-renowned department store? Excellent benefits. Store room attendants and organisers start at £8,000 per annum. Management trainees will begin their careers on £14,000 per annum. Apply in writing only to: PO Box 111, London.

Although there are no stated qualification requirements in the advertisement, you can assume that different levels of applicants are sought. It could well be that the management trainees are expected to have a degree or 'A'-levels with some relevant part-time work experience. The store room attendants and organisers can offer less qualified individuals an entry. With hard work and determination they could be the management trainee of the future.

Deciding on your preferred type and style of organisation
When reviewing the style of any organisation you will want to consider a number of aspects:

- size of the organisation; is it large, medium or small

- ownership; this can mean public or private sector as well as which country owns the company

- is it listed on the stock market of its country of origin

- industry sector; whether it is in the services, manufacturing or retail sector

- emphasis of organisation; is it forward-thinking, change-orientated, traditional, etc.

Reviewing the preferred area to work

At this point it may be necessary to review your chosen work location. As long as you have chosen your accommodation sensibly this should not prove an issue because travelling around central London is reasonably straightforward.

Considering your priorities

The identification of a broad range of possible avenues to investigate is normal. However, you will undoubtedly have a preference and this should be your main focus of attention, at least in the initial stages of the job search.

The realities of today's job market will mean that you will have to make compromises. London is a competitive environment. Keeping realistic and flexible are the main keys to success in London and if you find that your preferred choice shows little or no sign of success, you must be ready and willing to alter direction.

This does not mean that you should just take any job. However, if your desired employment is going to take longer to achieve or requires you to attain additional qualifications and/or experience then you may want to consider temporary work, or possibly your second choice, until you can achieve your ultimate goal.

UNDERSTANDING THE MARKETS

A positive starting point is to draw up a list of possible companies which you are interested in working for. This is relatively straightforward once your analysis of opportunities has been completed. You will then need to focus your mind on the precise detail of your preferences:

- specific industry sector
- size and ownership of the company
- level of position sought
- name, if possible, and title of the person that position reports to or the relevant personnel (Human Resources) name.

Sources of information

There is a multitude of sources of information. Most of these can be found in the many libraries in and around London. Wherever you live in London there will be a library close by. Consult your local telephone directory.

Two of the best are:

Westminster Reference Library	City Business Library
35 St Martin's Street	1 Brewer's Hall Garden
London	Off Aldermanbury Square
W.C2H 7HP	London EC2V 5BX
Tel: (020) 7641 4634	Tel: (020) 7638 8215/6
Tube: Leicester Square	Tube: Bank or St Paul's

The following books and information can be found in most good reference libraries:

CEPEC Recruitment Guide and Executive Grapevine (annual)
Two reference books listing recruitment and employment agencies throughout the country. It gives industry specialisations and background information.

Kompass UK Trade Names
Lists approximately 55,000 active trade names, with a brief description and company information.

Times 1000
This is an annual financial review of leading UK companies. There are individual sections on nationalised industries, banks, foreign banks, insurance companies and building societies in Britain.

Stock Exchange Official Yearbook
Provides financial information and names of directors of all UK Stock Exchange quoted companies.

The Personnel Manager's Yearbook
This is an annual reference book detailing Personnel and Human Resource departments in major UK organisations. It lists the top contact names within the companies.

Britain's Top Private Companies
Lists information about private companies.

Extel
This is a statistical card service giving financial information on quoted companies and a selection of unquoted companies. When reviewing this information take care that it is the most recent available.

McCarthy Cards
For information prior to an interview you can read all recent items published in international newspapers and journals on quoted and unquoted companies.

Newspapers and trade journals
Daily newspapers and current trade journals are on display.

Other effective sources of information are:

Internet
Access to the Internet can prove an invaluable source of information and unlike books and the annual reports and accounts of companies, it gives the most recent published information.

Telephone directories
Never underestimate the usefulness of the local telephone directories:

- the *Yellow Pages* will give details of companies by industry sector with address and telephone number

- the *Greater London Business Directory* gives an alphabetical list of companies with addresses and telephone numbers.

Annual reports and accounts
Although there will be a selection of reports and accounts available at a good reference library, you will find that these can easily be obtained by telephoning the marketing department of the company in question. The facts and figures offer a guide to the financial state of the company, but one of the most important sections to read is the chairman's review and mission statement, usually at the front of the booklet. This will give you an indication of the direction the company intends to take in the future.

Product catalogues and leaflets
Request up-to-date product or service leaflets, either by telephoning or visiting the premises of your targeted firms. This will give you an insight into the business of the company. In addition, if you can speak to any of the suppliers or customers of an organisation, you will gain a further understanding of how the company works and what it is like to work with.

Seeking out information about potential employers
The importance of researching a company cannot be stressed enough. The more information you have about a potential employer the more likely you are to get a job with them. All employers want prospective employees to show an interest in the organisation that is considering recruiting and paying them.

Even a small business will set high standards in quality products and customer care. It will want to portray the right image and likes to feel it is getting its message across. Being able to comment on some positive aspect of a company's activities produces a positive reaction and will always work to your advantage.

Put yourself in their position – who would you rather recruit; a person who knows about the industry sector and the company in detail; or someone who knows nothing about it?

You will be competing with the best, so intelligent comments and questions about the firm, at every stage, will be expected.

Keeping current
Another significant way to show yourself in a better light than the competition is to have an excellent general knowledge of current business news. It is sensible to read at least one daily broadsheet newspaper, the *Financial Times* on Saturday and a serious Sunday newspaper, to keep yourself up to date. The London paper to buy is the *Evening Standard*, which is available Monday to Friday afternoons.

The cost of buying newspapers can be reduced by using your local library, which will have most of them available each day.

REVIEWING OPPORTUNITIES

With a great deal of hard work, professionalism, research and a little luck you could have a choice of job offers. Whether or not this is the case there will be important questions you need to ask yourself before accepting any job offer. With more than one offer you will need to compare your answers carefully.

1. Is the job specification to your requirement?

2. How do you feel about your prospective employers, colleagues and subordinates?

3. Do they have the career development plan you are looking for?

4. Is the salary within the range specified?

5. Is the location acceptable relating to commuting distance?

6. Does the job involve travel? If so, how much? Is this acceptable?

Whatever the situation, always read the contract thoroughly and never sign anything unless you are:

- sure of the meaning
- happy with it.

Negotiating the position

If the offer is close to your ideal but one or two aspects are unsatisfactory, you may consider it worth trying to negotiate to gain a more acceptable contract. There are advantages and disadvantages to this.

Advantages
- If handled professionally, your future employer may be impressed with your style.

- If you eventually accept the contract without amendment, after negotiation, it can indicate your flexibility of approach to your new employer.

- One or two alterations can give you additional encouragement to perform well in your new role.

Disadvantages
- There may be other people ready and willing to take the job as it stands.

- The firm may be unable to alter any aspect of the contract as a matter of consistency with current employees.

- If handled badly you could appear arrogant.

Whether you are successful or not will depend on a number of things:

1. The type of market place you are in. If you are an expert in your field you have a greater chance of success in amending the terms of an employment contract.

2. How you approach the negotiation. You will need to use tact and diplomacy.

3. How flexible the company's contracts are allowed to be.

KNOWING THE WORK ENVIRONMENT

Before starting in your new job you will need to consider how you will be expected to behave as an employee. Even before you arrive for your first day you will need to have certain things planned.

Your journey to work
It is essential that you try the journey in rush hour. As explained, a journey during rush hour will be much slower than at other times of the day and you must ensure you arrive on time. Travelling around London requires practise.

Your work clothes
Plan what you will be wearing, at least for the first few days. You should have picked up the style and dress code from your interview. If in doubt wear a business suit. It is always better to overdress.

Your travel pass
One of the most time-consuming aspects of any journey, especially on a Monday morning, can be queueing for a ticket to travel. Plan ahead and purchase a seven-day ticket. This can be done the previous evening to save time and hassle. You will need a pass with your photograph; so get yourself organised.

Attitude
One criterion for success will depend on your attitude towards your new role and colleagues. It is important to listen, work hard and ask questions. Never be afraid to take notes when you are being given instructions. It is an excellent way to show your professionalism. If you are unsure of anything, always ask.

In a new job it is always advisable to keep your head down and work hard. It will take a few months before you understand the structure and politics of any organisation.

Patience
Always stay patient with other people, showing professionalism. In addition show patience with yourself. You will be in a totally new

environment, surrounded by new faces, doing a new job. Give yourself time.

WORKING AS A TEMPORARY

A temporary job is a clever way to receive cash, usually on a weekly basis, whilst allowing the flexibility and time to go for interviews for permanent positions. There is a large temporary job market in London.

Advantages of temporary work

1. Potential permanent employers will be impressed by your willingness to work.

2. Temporary work can be enjoyable because, even if the assignment is dull, you will be in a new environment with a different set of people – all potential new friends. This, in itself, can prove a stimulus and help you settle into London life.

3. The knowledge that you will not be in the job for long prevents it from becoming too mundane.

4. Temporary positions frequently develop into permanent positions, either because a different vacancy occurs within the firm or the position you are currently covering becomes available on a permanent contract.

5. Temporary positions are quicker to get than permanent jobs as less time is taken checking references and background.

6. It may give you an opportunity to work in the industry sector of your choice, even though you are unable to get a permanent position in it at present.

7. Temporary work assists cash-flow immediately as payment is normally made each week, which can be useful when facing the expense of moving.

8. You will have an opportunity, without long-term commitment, to assess if this is your desired career.

Disadvantages of temporary work

1. A temporary assignment below your qualifications and capabilities can signal to a potential permanent employer that you are at a lower level than you actually are.

2. You will need to take care when detailing this period of work on your CV.

3. Temporary work can be busy and hectic and you may forget or be unable to continue your proper job search.

4. You could be offered a permanent position and take it even though it is not your ideal simply because it is easier and quicker than looking for another job.

5. There is a strong possibility that you will be given the tasks which no permanent employee wants to do.

Availability

A firm may use temporary employees for any of the following reasons:

- an employee is taking maternity leave and may or may not be returning

- one or more employees are on holiday and specialist cover is needed

- the firm is expanding rapidly and has yet to recruit enough qualified staff

- the firm, for whatever reason, is unsure of exactly the type and level of employee needed to fill the vacancy

- there are seasonal fluctuations within the industry

- the firm always prefers to use a percentage of temporaries because it cuts down on other costs; e.g. holiday pay, benefits, etc.

- there is a large contract which has to be fulfilled in a short space of time

- the firm has a high turnover of staff because it is an unpleasant place to work.

Temporary work is available in a broad range of industries and many high street agencies deal with these vacancies. There are some agencies which specialise only in temporary positions. Temporary positions are seldom found in the local or national press because of the cost of advertising.

An agency can specialise in any of the following areas:

- accountancy and book-keeping

- receptionists and telephonists

- secretarial and personal assistants

- chefs and catering

- administrative and clerical

- telesales and marketing

- legal locums

- proofreading and editing

- back office settlements in banking.

For example: if you began your working life as a secretary or receptionist but have since moved into management it may be possible to go back to secretarial or receptionist work as a temporary. One point you need to be aware of is that under the Employment Agencies Act, an agency must test your skills. Therefore, it is essential that you practise these skills before going to see the agency, especially if they are rusty.

If this whole concept is new to you it may be sensible to consider visiting one or two of the smaller agencies to begin with. The smaller agency is more likely to give you the time and guidance needed to set you on your way. This will give you an insight into the way they all operate.

Timing of approach
Most firms contact temporary agencies with their requirements at the end of each week for a booking to start the following week. As a consequence the most productive days to visit or contact an agency are Thursday or Friday. You may find that the busiest agencies, once you have signed on with them, will ask you not to call them. They will insist on contacting you. You must understand that if they are busy you will do yourself no favours by calling them.

Making the most of reliability
The temporary sector is notorious for being unreliable, so a visit or telephone call on a Monday morning can prove to be beneficial. You may be able to pick up a booking where another person has become unavailable by calling in 'sick'.

This means that you can easily show yourself to be as good or better than the majority by being reliable and efficient.

CHECKLIST

1. Find or arrange access to the Internet and other suitable equipment.

2. Seek out information at your local library and assess the information available.

3. Contact your target companies for annual report and accounts and any product or service leaflets available.

4. Consider the possibility of temporary work by contacting a few agencies.

5. Keep up to date by reading the daily newspapers and relevant trade journals.

7

Working in the City

The objective of this chapter is to give you a plain and simple guide to what the City of London is all about. It takes a look at the institutions which operate there to help you understand any career opportunities. If you are considering building a career in this individualistic arena then you need to be prepared to work hard and play hard.

Perhaps at least one clarification is needed relating to the title 'the City'. This title tends to be used mainly by those who actually work there and is not intended to infer that this is the only 'City' anywhere or that this is the only centre of financial expertise in a major city.

The institutions based within the City employ approximately 350,000 people. This number has declined during the last 15 years from over 500,000. The vast majority of these workers are employed by the banking and finance sector and are office workers. The remainder work for services provided to the workers in that sector. The City or 'Square Mile', as it is often referred to, has its own special atmosphere and work ethic.

WHAT IS MEANT BY THE CITY

Situation

The City is not a square, despite its nickname. It is more like a odd-shaped rectangle. Inside its narrow area there are a variety of financial markets and specialists, all within a short walking distance of each other. You can walk from one end of the City to the other in approximately 20 minutes, if you know your way around. There are many narrow streets, which can make you feel as if you are in a rabbit warren, leading from area to area. The direction you are walking can be misleading at the best of times.

Its position is as follows:

- to the west of the City is Temple Bar and Holborn Bar, with

London's centre for the legal profession and Law Courts as well as Fleet Street which traditionally housed the national newspapers (they have moved east in recent years to the Docklands area)

- Moorfields and Smithfields Meat Market are both to the north
- Aldgate and Tower Hill are to the East
- the River Thames is to the south.

Who runs it

It is ruled by the Lord Mayor of London and the City of London Corporation. The City of London Corporation has the same powers as any other London borough, but with some additional authority. The most notable addition is its own police force.

An example of its special powers was shown immediately after the IRA bomb which devastated the NatWest Tower and surrounding buildings in 1992. The Corporation of London police placed a ring around the City by stopping and searching every vehicle which tried to enter. This was kept in place until the IRA ceasefire.

However, the financial institutions which operate from the City are policed by:

- the Bank of England
- the Securities and Futures Authority (SFA)
- the Investment Management Regulatory Organisation (IMRO)
- the Securities and Investment Board (SIB)
- Financial Intermediaries, Managers & Brokers Regulatory Association (FIMBRA)
- Life Assurance and Unit Trust Regulatory Organisation (LAUTRO).

The institutions based there

Apart from working in the City there are numerous places to visit, and most of them are free to enter, including many buildings with celebrated architecture as well as interesting activities to watch. If you wish to work in the City then go and visit these institutions to find out as much information as you can. They are covered in more detail in Chapter 9.

As a brief guide to the City follow this plan:

1. Take the underground to Bank station and follow the exit to the Bank of England.

2. The Royal Exchange building is opposite the Bank of England.
3. Continue down Threadneedle Street and the Stock Exchange is on your left-hand side as you enter Old Broad Street.
4. Continue to the bottom of Old Broad Street for the Broadgate centre, home to many banks with an ice-rink at its centre.
5. Either walk or take the tube to Monument station where you can find the London Metal Exchange in Leadenhall Street.
6. Lloyds of London is in Lime Street, with its architecturally controversial building.
7. Further along, the Baltic Exchange in St Mary Axe has a new home after the IRA bomb in 1992.
8. A short walk to Cannon Street will bring you to the former LIFFE building.

In addition to this area the Docklands development has become home to many British and American banks during the last few years – despite its difficult beginnings. The main decision-making institutions, such as the Bank of England are still based in the 'Square Mile' and are unlikely to move. However, public transport is now being improved to the Docklands area, and with the extension of the Jubilee line Docklands is likely to remain an important home for financial institutions in the future.

The City is still one of the world's great financial centres. It is the pivotal point for world trade in commodities, even though most of these raw goods do not originate in the United Kingdom. You will see from the history and background how each of the major institutions developed and how they function today.

HISTORY AND BACKGROUND

The history of the City can be traced back centuries and many of those who work there have little understanding of its past. Until the 1980s it was a relatively unregulated environment, working on the principle that: 'my word is my bond'.

Although this principle still exists, there are many more regulations in place now. Critics still say that these regulations are still not stringent enough as there is still a heavy reliance on self-regulation. This was especially true after the collapse of Barings Bank in 1995. The collapse was due to one 'rogue' trader, Nick Leeson, whose deals and debts were not monitored or understood by Barings management.

The beginnings
The Romans originally developed the area known as the City. They withdrew from Britain in 410 AD. The area was originally enclosed by a wall with six gates:

- Bishopsgate
- Moorgate
- Ludgate
- Aldgate
- Newgate
- Aldersgate

In the 17th century, London became the centre for a mass of economic activity, much of it as a consequence of being one of Europe's largest trading ports.

As trade continued to develop, voyages became longer. Individuals were not prepared to put their money into such long-term ventures up-front and without security and so, in the 18th century, entrepreneurs began to meet in coffee houses to find finance for the projects. In addition, shares in these projects could be exchanged or even sold.

Continuing the development
It wasn't until 1802 that the Stock Exchange was actually formed to provide a method of completing these transactions in a regulated form. Naturally the major British and international banks based themselves close by for convenience to these borrowers. Lombard Street developed into the main banking street.

Stock Exchange (1912–86)
The Stock Exchange continued to develop. Its main system of operating for over 70 years was known as 'single capacity dealing' with fixed commissions. It went as follows:

1. The first step to investing was for an individual to approach a stockbroker who, with his or her access to the market and knowledge of companies, would give advice on those companies which he or she believed to be a good investment.

2. The choice of what to buy would be left to the individual whilst taking into account the stockbroker's recommendations.

3. When the stockbroker had been given the order he or she would approach different stockjobbers on the floor of the Stock Exchange to ask prices without letting on whether he or she was buying or selling.

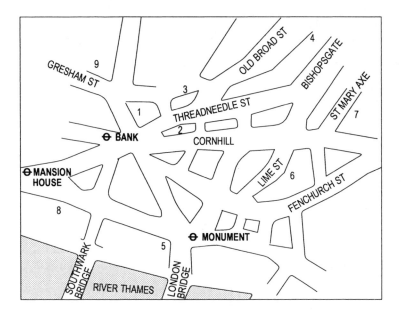

Key:

1 Bank of England
2 Royal Exchange
3 Stock Exchange
4 NatWest Tower
5 Fishmongers' Hall

6 Lloyds
7 Baltic Exchange
8 Vintner's Hall
9 Guildhall

Fig. 6. Map of the City of London.

4. The jobber would give two prices. The lowest price quoted would be for the jobber to buy and the broker to sell, and the highest price for the jobber to sell and the broker to buy. These are known as bid-and-offer prices.

5. The stockbroker would find the jobber who was selling at the lowest price and return to him or her to purchase the shares on behalf of his client. Clearly the opposite would be true if the broker was selling.

The system worked well initially, with the broker obliged to get the best possible price for the client, and the jobber compelled to trade with the broker once a price had been quoted. 'Single capacity' indicated that each of the stockbroker and stockjobber had a single function.

Stock Exchange (1986 to present day)
Although this system had worked well, a process for change was initiated in 1983 which would abolish the minimum commissions and single capacity, opening up the market to new members. Several factors were taken into account before the process of change was agreed.

1. As technology and computerisation were developing rapidly they were deemed essential as a provider of information as well as to be able to deal via computer.

2. The fixed commissions in operation meant that many London-based brokers were re-routing their business through other stock exchanges around the world as the other exchanges had commissions which were negotiable and consequently cheaper.

3. Some UK companies saw more trading of their shares in New York than in London.

4. The Conservative government, at the time, believed that the fixed commissions were inhibiting the Stock Market from continuing to develop.

The change was implemented on 27 October 1987 and is known as the 'Big Bang'. Almost one year later, on 19 October 1988, the stock markets throughout the world suffered one of the largest crashes ever recorded – a day known as 'Black Monday'. These two events are not considered to be connected, although they shaped the market.

Current trading
Today there is no 'trading floor'. The 'market makers', as they are now called, can act on behalf of clients as agents, as well as holding shares in quoted companies themselves. They now have more than one function.

In addition, there are still many firms which operate on the simple basis of only buying and selling shares for clients.

A new computer system for settling all of these trades was introduced in 1994, known as CREST. This system replaced the ill-fated TAURUS which could not offer the speed of transfer necessary for the new market.

Bank of England
The Bank of England was established in 1694. The original governing body, known as the Court of Directors, consisted of a governor, deputy governor and 24 directors. When it was nationalised in 1946 the number of directors was reduced to 16.

The directors meet each Wednesday (moved from Thursday). Since the Labour government came to power in 1997 the Bank of England has been given 'independence' to set interest rates without government intervention.

Here are some of the major functions of the Bank of England:

1. The banker to the government. It holds the government's main bank account and will borrow on behalf of the government by issuing government-backed securities.

2. The banker to the banking sector. It holds bank accounts of the clearing banks and other financial institutions, including overseas central banks and the International Monetary Fund (IMF).

3. It issues the country's bank notes.

4. It is responsible for the supervision of the financial services sector.

5. It acts as a contact point for other central financial institutions.

6. It advises the government on monetary policy and carries it out by intervening in the markets when necessary.

LIFFE
The London International Financial Futures and Options Exchange opened in 1982. Despite the fact it was still a comparatively new market, its position was first in Europe, third in the world and it offered a bigger diversity of financial and commodity contracts than either New York or Chicago – the latter being the first financial futures exchange to open.

To become a member of LIFFE a firm needed to buy a 'seat', when available. A seat allowed a firm to trade on the floor by 'open outcry' or, more accurately, by shouting at each other. Members included:

- banks, British and overseas
- brokers
- overseas private owners
- securities houses.

The contracts traded on LIFFE required the delivery of a commodity, currency or security in a specified future month, if the transaction was not liquidated prior to that date. In reality delivery rarely, if ever, took place. These futures were traded as follows:

1. An order was placed to the LIFFE member, either by telephone, fax or e-mail. The order was written out and time-stamped.
2. From the 'seat' or booth a runner (in a yellow jacket) took the slip to a trader who was on the floor or 'trading pit'.
3. The trader, who was wearing a bright-coloured jacket unique to the firm he or she worked for, would carry out the order by a combination of shouting and designated hand signals.
4. When the order was complete the details were written on the original order slip and confirmed to the client.

All transactions were monitored and reported. The system in place allowed real-time information to be available throughout the world.

In 1999 LIFFE was completely reinvented and now exists solely as an electronic trading platform – LIFFE CONNECT™.

London Metal Exchange
The London Metal Exchange operates from 56 Leadenhall Street. There is an independent board of directors which is responsible for the exchange trading the seven metals:

- aluminium
- aluminium alloy
- nickel
- tin
- copper
- lead
- zinc.

The trading takes place between 11.45 and 13.25, and 15.20 and 17.00 by the 17 ring dealer members present. The members are mainly overseas companies.

London Commodity Exchange
Based in St Katharine's Dock, the London Commodity Exchange now administers the Baltic Futures Market. The Exchange is a main international trading centre for soft commodities, such as cocoa and sugar. It also trades in BIFFEX, which is the shipping freight rate index.

Lloyds of London
In 1688 Edward Lloyd opened his coffee shop in Tower Street as a
base for merchants to conduct their business. Since that date Lloyds
of London has developed into a unique market. It is not an
insurance company but a series of syndicates which are financed by:

- names; private individuals who have unlimited liability
- corporate members which trade with limited liability.

In order to be considered a 'name' you must have at least £250,000
disposable income and lodge considerable funds with Lloyds.
During the 1980s and early 1990s many Lloyds 'names' were
declared bankrupt due to the enormous insurance losses incurred.
Reforms took place, with Lloyds emerging from loss in 1993. The
scope of Lloyds is now huge. It covers:

- offshore oil and gas exploration
- space technology
- road transport
- aviation
- marine (its original business).

Baltic Exchange
Moved to St Mary Axe after the IRA bomb in 1992 destroyed its
original building, it operates a shipping exchange. Members include:

- ship-owners
- ship-brokers
- maritime lawyers
- others involved in shipping.

REVIEWING THE FINANCIAL SERVICES SECTOR

Up until the 1980s each banking institution had its own specialist
area and knowledge. There was a tradition, built over many years,
with many small merchant banks and stockbrokers retaining their
original specialisations.

As the markets evolved after 'Big Bang' and the subsequent fall
out following 'Black Monday', the dividing lines between functions
and specialist markets became less clear. In many cases it
disappeared completely. Many people moved jobs. Many mergers

and acquisitions took place between a variety of financial institutions to provide large firms who can offer every aspect of the financial market.

The business carried on in the City continues to change and alter according to market needs.

The continuing changes mean:

- job opportunities come and go rapidly

- careers and jobs continually alter

- new financial instruments are regularly brought into the market

- keeping up to date is of primary importance

- new markets are being invented all the time

- the mergers have reduced staff by approximately 30 per cent over the last 15 years.

ASSESSING THE VARIETY OF CAREERS AVAILABLE

As you will have seen by now the City means more than simply working in a bank such as in your local high street branch. Banking in the city means something totally different. Here are some other career options in the City to consider:

- secretary
- accountant
- lawyer
- financial consultant
- stockbroker
- company secretary
- tax consultant
- insurance broker
- insurance underwriter
- investment analyst
- computer programmer
- actuary
- broker

- auditor
- recruitment consultant
- human resources
- training and development
- careers' adviser
- financial journalist
- traditional banking
- investment banking
- regulatory supervisor
- taxi driver
- trader
- dealer
- personal assistant

and many others.

DO YOU HAVE WHAT IT TAKES?

So what does it take to develop a career in the City?

That will depend on what it is you want to do and how long for. If one or more ideas from the above information and list appeal to you then think carefully and begin your research. You may want a successful career trying to get to the top of your chosen area, or you may simply want to work there without aspiring to great heights. Both ends of the spectrum are possible as well as all levels along the way.

Review the following aspects and decide how you need to approach each of them.

Education and qualifications

Throughout the country there are owners of companies without academic qualifications and there are filing clerks with degrees. A definitive answer to the right type of qualifications needed for a successful career in the City is impossible to give. Whatever the level you have attained you can succeed. You may find this guide helpful.

1. The higher your qualifications the better chance you have in getting the initial interview, in theory. You need to bear in mind that the City, like all places, will have a mixture of people at all levels. It may just be that the person recruiting you started out with few, or even no qualifications, and will jump at the opportunity to give motivated individuals the same chance that was bestowed on them.

2. Keep realistic when applying for positions because even the most motivated individual is unlikely to be given an opening on a graduate trainee programme with only one GCSE.

3. Although the City is known as an industry sector where 'jobs for the boys' is talked about as being commonplace, this is less true today. Of course it still exists. So, if you do know anyone who works there, it is time to put your new-found networking skills into practice.

Energy, enthusiasm and determination

The measurement of your energy, enthusiasm and determination levels are something which only you will know. However, you need to learn how to portray these to the person or persons reading your CV and interviewing you.

There is a fine line between allowing your determination to shine through and appearing arrogant. Here are some hints:

- always keep your CV professional and up to date
- avoid phrases such as, 'I know I'm the best person for the job because...'
- always dress appropriately, business suits (not brown) are essential in the City
- ensure that you have done your research so that you can ask sensible questions
- never assume anything.

Job search skills
You will have started your development of these skills after reviewing Chapter 5. An important point to bear in mind is that, as with any skill, job search skills will improve with practice. Remember this and do not begin your job search by putting all your efforts into your ideal position. Have a practice run on a firm or position which may not be your first choice.

Background
The City is full of people from all types of background. Most individuals will tell you that they are proud of where they come from. You will usually find someone from a similar background to yourself and this can prove a great source of inspiration.

Never be embarrassed or concerned about discussing your background. Keep an open mind.

Market knowledge and understanding
Arriving in the City for the first time from another part of the country, or from overseas means that you are unlikely to have a full knowledge and understanding of how it operates, however much you read. It is essential to build this up. Some suggestions:

- watch relevant business programmes on television
- visit the area and the actual institutions (see Chapter 9)
- talk to anyone you know who works there or who has worked there
- keep in touch by reading the business press
- spend time on the Internet.

Focus

You need to keep focused during your job search. This can prove difficult at times. One of the most productive ways to keep yourself in touch with what is going on in the City is to stick to a rigid timetable which will be good practice for when you get your job. An example of such a timetable could be:

DAY	MORNING	AFTERNOON
Monday	Visit library, research	Structure three direct approach letters
Tuesday	Visit library, review papers for job advertisements	Reply to appropriate advertisements
Wednesday	Visit City institution	Call direct on three firms
Thursday	Review papers	Reply to appropriate advertisements
Friday	Telephone recruitment agencies	Respond to any letters and replies

Clothes and accessories

A list of essentials:

- at least one business suit – dark grey, black, navy blue – definitely not brown (especially men) in the City

- a smart, small briefcase

- accessories to match the suit, shoes, etc.

- white, blue, cream shirts or blouses

- if male, a few sensible silk ties

- an accurate watch.

STARTING AT THE BOTTOM

If you have reviewed the options available and determined that a career in the City is for you, then go for it. Whatever your background and qualifications there are options available to you. So here are some suggestions on starting at the bottom:

- research your target organisations with a view to beginning your career as a junior by finding out what a junior would do within that firm

- study the sector in detail, spending most of your spare time taking additional relevant qualifications, such as the Chartered Institute of Bankers examinations

- always show an interest in your job and be willing to work hard and take on extra tasks

- do not be frightened to show your knowledge

- always dress as the person who is your direct superior

- keep alert and take in as much information as you can at all times.

CHECKLIST

1. Research the types of firms and careers which operate in the City.

2. Ask advice from any friends who work in the City.

3. Spend time and as much money as your budget will allow on organising your wardrobe appropriately.

4. Arrange to visit one or more of the institutions mentioned (see Chapter 9).

5. Work out a structured timetable.

8

Settling In

Settling in to a new home and new area takes time and can be an anxious experience. The difficulties of learning where everything is from scratch, combined with making new friends and acquaintances, not to mention starting a new job, can cause much anguish. Initially, you will not know many people, if anyone. You will not know the location of:

- shops
- restaurants
- bus stops or tube stations
- supermarkets
- doctors, dentists, etc.

There is a multitude of things you can do to assist with the transition. You need to plan in order to give yourself a head start.

1. Allow yourself time and do not expect to know everything overnight. Allow plenty of time when travelling around.

2. Read as much relevant background information as you can before the actual move takes place by getting all of the local papers and any leaflets about the locality.

3. When you finally move in try to keep up to date by watching the local television news, listening to one of London's many radio stations and reading local newspapers and magazines. A list of newspapers and magazines is given towards the end of the book.

4. During daylight hours spend time walking around from area to area. This will give you a sense of where areas and districts are in relation to each other and their differences.

5. Try to remain open-minded.

6. Be inquisitive and ask questions about different areas.

7. If you are lucky enough to know someone who has lived in London for a time, or still does, ask them to show you around.

8. Take time out to listen to others' advice.

9. Develop an understanding of the culture of the area you live and work in.

UNDERSTANDING THE CULTURE

Understanding the culture of the area will be of great help to you as you begin to settle in. Culture has several meanings and can refer to the arts, literature, painting, theatre and opera, but can also be defined as the way of life of a particular group of people, including every aspect of what that group thinks, says and does. Culture refers to systems of attitudes, values and feelings which are learned, inherited or passed down from generation to generation. It is the customs, civilisation and achievements of a particular time or people.

You will be moving into a different culture when you move to London, and this in itself can be difficult to acclimatise to. In addition, each area of London has its own individual customs, and, some would say, culture. These customs can vary dramatically from another area which may be only two miles away.

Cultural differences

Sceptics would have you believe that London has no overall culture, for two reasons:

● there is such a wide cross-section of people who now consider it to be 'home'

● there is a transient population which is not only diverse from area to area but can change totally within one area in a short period of time.

Although these reasons are true to a certain extent, they are not the whole story. These differences and alterations can be seen clearly but they are not new to Londoners. London has seen a wide variety of people for many years now. It is also true that many other large cities, especially capital cities, around the world have these same issues. Some of the issues which can affect culture are:

- racial differences

- gender and sexual orientation differences

- disparities in financial backgrounds and expectations

- religious differences.

Trend-setting
Culture and customs should not be confused with trend-setting. There will always be areas in London which are known as 'trendy'. These change frequently and sometimes depend on a famous pop star or film star moving to the area.

Cultural similarities
It is not until people from these varying backgrounds meet that we discover the similarities between the cultures. These are seldom highlighted. Human nature shows many similarities, whichever walk of life you are from. Cultural differences combined with a common purpose gives the Londoner a determination and, some would say, hostile attitude. It is better defined as an attitude of surviving in a sometimes unfriendly and fast-paced atmosphere. Consider the following:

- attitudes to pollution and the environment

- sentiments about public transport

- striving to achieve a better living standard

- beliefs that people can all work together.

The vast majority of individuals who choose London as their home – even if only for a relatively short period of time – strive for a better way of life, not just for themselves but for everyone living there. So how can you fit into the culture? Here are a few ideas:

1. Always understand that each individual has a right to their own beliefs and attitudes, together with a right to express these views.

2. When meeting people, especially for the first time, try to find a common ground for discussion.

3. Try not to judge others on their appearance, dress code and views.

4. Spend some time researching different religions and faiths. This will help to move forward conversations.

5. Put your own opinions forward in an assertive manner, not an aggressive one.

6. Ensure you keep any biased or unsympathetic opinions to yourself.

7. Be willing to ask questions and listen to other people's answers and views.

8. Avoid becoming involved with aggressive groups which do not listen to other's opinions.

ADJUSTING TO EXPECTATIONS

When you first move you are likely to spend the first few months adjusting to the pace of life and culture. You may find that friends and family from your home area will put added pressure on you with their expectations. This will be for a wide variety of reasons:

1. A genuine concern that you are living in the capital city on your own, with all the difficulties that entails. It may well be that any bad publicity about violence relating to London will result in a telephone call from close relatives to ensure that you are well. Be sensitive to their concerns. The incident may have occurred a long way from where you live and work. They may not understand that. They could need reassurance.

2. A sense of wanting you to do well. They may expect that within a short period of time you will have made your fortune! Be patient with relatives and friends and try to instil patience in them. If you take time to keep them informed they will respond by giving you more space. Try to write or telephone on a regular basis.

3. A sense of jealousy in that they are not the one setting off on such an exciting journey. Try to include them in your own personal journey, whenever you can.

Whatever attitude they take, you may find it can become irritating or at least tiring after only a short period of time. Try not to be confrontational. You need to understand and remember that they have no idea what you are going through. You need to be able to explain this with care. The more you keep them informed, the more likely they are to stay calm.

London can appear a frightening and hostile environment to

those who do not know it. You may need to show maturity and consideration, especially with parents. It can be an excellent idea to invite them to visit you, if you handle it carefully. Contemplate the advantages and disadvantages of such an invitation:

Advantages
- it will give them an insight into your living and working conditions

- they will have an opportunity to meet your friends and possibly some of your work colleagues

- your future discussions with them can be focused on people they have met and areas which they have visited

- they can take heart in the fact that you are looking after yourself.

Disadvantages
- if they see you are not caring for yourself it could have the adverse effect to the one you want and could increase the number of telephone calls

- you will need to give the visit your undivided attention, putting aside time from your settling-in process.

BATTLING WITH HOMESICKNESS

Homesickness can be defined as being depressed by longing for one's home during an absence from it. Although you may feel that this is a sentimental attitude and unlikely to happen to you, consider the following points. Will you ever feel:

- you are pining for a close friend to share a particular experience, either good or bad

- nostalgic for those things in life which you have grown up with and which have surrounded you for many years

- wistful of aspects of your life which are no longer around you all day and night

- a sense of loneliness to share a secret or adventure with a person you know very well

- a sense that you just want an evening in with group of people who have known you all your life and with whom you can simply relax.

The truth of the matter is that most people feel at least one of these emotions at some time when absent from home for an extended period of time. Do not hide away from the feeling, face up to it.

Facing up to homesickness
Each individual will treat homesickness differently. Here are some alternatives:

- visit your home for a few days and go out and about with your close friends and relatives

- ask your friend(s) and relatives to visit you

- if you are unable to visit friends or relatives or have them visit you talk things through with a new-found friend who will probably have experienced something similar at some point

- telephone the people you miss most

- write to people or send an e-mail message as a way to start up an ongoing contact.

FINDING YOUR FEET

When you finally find your feet you will feel a buzz. The time it will take will vary from person to person. The process will happen gradually but you will know it has happened when:

- you have plenty of social engagements without making any special effort

- you are the one explaining to others where to meet and how to get there

- you do not have to look at the tube map to get around, and you know instinctively where to stand on the underground platform for a speedy exit at your destination stop

- you find yourself being asked which are the good restaurants and bars to go to.

When this time arrives remember that there will be those people around who are just starting to try to find their way.

DEVELOPING NEW RELATIONSHIPS

Friendships and relationships will need to be built. This is usually a gradual process. You will need to spend time on developing emotional associations. When young it comes naturally as, generally, children have fewer inhibitions. As people grow and develop they place their own beliefs and prejudices on the shoulders of others. This makes developing new friendships more difficult.

London offers a multitude of choices of friends and, as explained earlier, from all backgrounds. There are friends for everyone. How do you find them?

1. If you have an interest or hobby which you have always wanted to learn more about, join an evening class. Each year a book called *Floodlight* is published which details all adult education courses available in London, both full- and part-time. The choice is massive and there is bound to be something there to interest you. It offers an opportunity to meet like-minded people.

2. Join a sports club or gymnasium. Once again you will find a large number of like-minded people with the added advantage you will get some regular exercise. You will find details in your local telephone directory. Many Londoners join a gym close to work as opposed to where they live as it can be more convenient to visit one during the lunch-hour.

3. Work colleagues are a great source of friendships and relationships. A vast number of those who live and work in London spend time with work colleagues.

4. Bars close to home or work are another option. You need to take care if going in alone. Always let someone know your whereabouts and when you will be home and if you change your plans always let them know.

5. Personal columns in the local or national newspapers often have a 'friends' column as well as a relationship column. If you arrange to meet anyone from this source always take great care. Meet in a public place, preferably during the day, and ensure that someone close to you knows exactly where you are going and who you are going to meet. This applies to all the meetings until you know the person well.

6. Work colleagues will have friends and family and you may be invited to parties or to meet them.

7. Occupants of the same building. You could easily find that the building you live in has a resident's meeting for all of the occupants of the flats every now and then. Go along, even if you have little to say. It will give you an opportunity to meet people.

8. Voluntary work, even of only for one or two hours every now and again, offers an excellent opportunity to meet people from different backgrounds.

CHECKLIST

1. Visit the local library to investigate the *Floodlight* book or buy it.

2. Review opportunities for voluntary work.

3. Discuss any problems with friends and relatives.

4. Keep family worries at bay by organising doctors, dentists and opticians as soon as possible.

9

Enjoying your Leisure Time

This chapter aims to give you a small selection of places to visit with brief background information as well as some ideas about what to do in your spare time. The choice in London is huge, but whenever you decide to go to see something specific it is usually worth telephoning in advance to check opening times and prices. Refurbishments, special events and theme evenings are common-place throughout the capital. They may result in the venue closing or prices increasing substantially.

One of the benefits of living in London is that there are so many great things to see. One of the best ways to visit the sights is with a group of people because frequently you can obtain discounts for larger numbers.

The following is not a definitive list, but a taster to get you started.

SOCIALISING ON A BUDGET

One of the most amazing aspects of London is that you can socialise on a budget. There are many free sights to see and you can save on transport costs by either walking or cycling. Other things to take into account are the numerous reasonably priced restaurants. You will soon find your own favourites as you spend more time socialising. Don't be afraid to venture out to new areas and try new places.

Eating out
Time Out's *Eating and Drinking Guide* is published every year and offers a separate section on each of the following as well as comprehensive coverage of most of London's restaurants:

- cafés
- pubs
- brasseries

- past restaurants
- pie and mash
- fish and chips

- wine bars
- pizza places
- budget eating.

- music bars
- vegetarian meals

For each restaurant the guide offers details on:

- estimated price for a meal

- cheapest wine whether house wine or the cheapest on the menu

- details of smoking and non-smoking areas

- detailed maps

- price of a glass of mineral water

- a summary of food laws.

A few of the more popular cheaper places to eat are:

Stockpot, 18 Old Compton Street, W1. Tel: (020) 7287 1066, offers cheap meals in a crowded, buzzing atmosphere. Note the following:

1. No credit cards are accepted.
2. A set meal of two courses is under £4.
3. House wine is approximately £6 per bottle.
4. Prices are cheaper before 17.00.

Café Emm, 17 Frith Street, W1. Tel: (020) 7437 0723, is a bustling café with loud music. Note the following:

1. No credit cards are accepted.
2. There is usually a young crowd with a party atmosphere.
3. House wine is approximately £9 per bottle.
4. A main course is between £5 and £7.

Sausage & Mash, 269 Portobello Road, W6. Tel: (020) 8968 8848, is a sit-down restaurant with a takeaway option. Note the following:

1. No credit cards are accepted.
2. Sausage, mash and gravy costs approximately £5.
3. Vegetarian option available.
4. House wine costs approximately £6 per bottle.

If you enjoy foods from around the world then there is a large choice in London:

1. There are many Chinese restaurants, although Chinatown in the West End is the best place to go for a choice which will fit all price ranges.

2. Indian restaurants abound, although Brick Lane in the East End offers the best choice.

3. Covent Garden offers a broad range of cafés and bars where you can eat and drink al-fresco.

4. In addition there are plenty of other nationalities to choose from, such as:
   English
   French
   Italian
   Mexican
   Vietnamese
   Ethiopian
   Caribbean
   Spanish.

Brunch
One popular way to meet with friends and enjoy a meal with a few drinks is to meet for brunch on Sundays. Many cafés around Hampstead and Little Venice offer a chance to sit outside as well. Café Laville on Edgware Road in Little Venice (W9) is situated over the canal and is a pleasant place to have Sunday brunch, followed by an afternoon at Lord's cricket ground.

Free things to do in London
There are plenty of free things to do in London, covering all aspects of life. Call the tourist information office for details. Here are a few possibilities:

Parks and gardens
Go to any of the parks and gardens. They are all free to enter (except for formal ones such as botanic gardens, Kew Gardens, etc.)

Outdoor sights
Visit outdoor sights such as Nelson's Column in Trafalgar Square,

Big Ben, the Cenotaph, Cleopatra's Needle, the Victoria Memorial, Eros and Piccadilly Circus, the Bradgate Centre, Smithfield Market, the Albert Memorial.

Churches

There are hundreds of churches in London that are free to enter. Most of them provide a fascinating insight into the history of the City. Try: St Martin-in-the-Fields, St Margaret's Westminster, Westminster Cathedral, St James' Church Piccadilly, All Hallows by the Tower, St Bride's Fleet Street, St Etheldreda's and Southwark Cathedral.

Law courts

There are four Inns of Court in Holborn, all of which are free to enter. This is where all of London's barristers work, but you can wander about at will.

Gray's Inn, Gray's Inn Road, WC1
Lincoln's Inn, Lincoln's Inn Fields, WC2
Middle Temple, Middle Temple Lane, EC4
Inner Temple, EC4.

Museums and galleries

Many of London's major museums and art galleries are free, although they appreciate donations. These are: Bank of England Museum, London Docklands Visitor Centre, Royal Naval College, Museum of Artillery, National Army Museum, Geffrye Museum, Percival David Foundation of Chinese Art, Museum of Garden History, Bethnal Green Museum of Childhood, Museum of Mankind, Keats' House, Leighton House Museum, Sir John Soane's Museum, William Morris Gallery, British Museum, National Gallery, National Portrait Gallery, Tate Gallery, Wallace Collection, Serpentine Gallery (Hyde Park).

Famous sights and events

Surprisingly some of London's most famous sights and events are free of charge: Ceremony of the Keys, Gun Salutes, Changing the Guard, Great Spitalfields Pancake Day Race, Oxford vs Cambridge Boat Race, London Harness Horse Parade, London Marathon (free to spectators), Swan Upping on the Thames, Notting Hill Carnival, Pearly Kings and Queens Festival, Punch & Judy Festival, State

Opening of Parliament, London to Brighton Veteran Car Run, Lord Mayor's Show, Christmas Lights in Trafalgar Square, New Year's Eve in Trafalgar Square, Chinese New Year Festival.

Window-shopping
As a last resort you could always try window-shopping! The best shops for interesting windows and displays are: Harrod's, Harvey Nichols, Fortnum & Mason, Dickins & Jones, Liberty and Selfridges.

APPRECIATING THE ARTS

Opera and ballet
Fans of opera and ballet will find a wide diversity of shows at any given time. Local newspapers give all details and current shows together with prices and timings.

Theatre
London's theatre life is the heart and soul of the capital's cultural life. There are some 40 commercial theatres, principally in the West End, as well as many fringe theatres. (Local, and some national newspapers give details of theatre performances, with prices and booking dates.) There are a few commercial theatres outside the West End:

- Mermaid in Puddle Dock
- Lyric in Hammersmith
- Old Vic at Waterloo.

There are two subsidised theatres:

- the National Theatre on the South Bank
- the Royal Shakespeare company at the Barbican.

All theatre tickets can be booked through the theatre's own booking office and the numerous ticket agents to be found throughout London – Ticketmaster (020) 7344 4444; First Call (020) 7497 9977. Be aware that many ticket agents will charge a booking fee. Full details are given in the local press and *Time Out* magazine (published weekly). Once again, you can usually obtain discounts for groups. However, for last-minute half-price tickets there is a booth situated in Leicester Square. It is easy to find as it has 'Ticket Booth' printed in large letters on its side. Tickets are available for that day's performances only and must be paid for in cash. During the tourist season it becomes exceptionally busy, so leave plenty of time to queue to buy your ticket.

Art galleries

London has many art galleries to visit. Always telephone before visiting to check the entrance price and opening hours, as these can change at short notice, particularly when a special exhibition is on.

Some of the major galleries are:

Courtauld Institute Galleries
Somerset House, Strand, WC2R 0RN
Tel: (020) 8873 2526
French Impressionist and post-Impressionist paintings.

Dulwich College Picture Gallery
College Road, SE21 7BG
Tel: (020) 8693 5254
Small collection of British, Dutch, Flemish, French and Italian paintings.

National Gallery
Trafalgar Square, WC2N 5DN
Tel: (020) 7839 3321
One of the finest national collections of western art.

Tate Gallery (moving to Bankside in 2000)
Millbank, SW1P 4RG
Tel: (020) 7887 8000
National collection of British art from 16–19th centuries as well as British, European, American paintings and sculpture.

Victoria and Albert Museum
Cromwell Road, SW7 5RL
Tel: (020) 7589 6371
Museum for applied and decorative arts. In addition there are collections of sculptures, miniatures and watercolours. It houses the largest representation of Constable's work.

Wallace Collection
Hertford House, Manchester Square, W1 2NP
Tel: (020) 7935 0687
Famous for 18th century French paintings.

Museums

London has over 200 museums and galleries to visit. Here are some points to bear in mind when you and your friends are trying to decide which to visit:

- always check opening times and prices

- arrive well before the time the museum is due to close to give yourself the opportunity to see everything

- if there is something you specifically want to see check it is still showing before visiting

- you may be able to get in free, depending upon circumstances

- you can purchase a London White Card, which allows unlimited access to 13 major museums and galleries over a period of three or seven days.

Some of the most important museums are:

British Museum
Great Russell Street, WC1
Tel: (020) 7636 1555

Cabinet War Rooms
Clive Steps
King Charles Street, SW1
Tel: (020) 7930 6961

Imperial War Museum
Lambeth Road, SE1
Tel: (020) 7416 5000

London Transport Museum
Covent Garden, WC2
Tel: (020) 7379 6344

Madame Tussaud's
Marylebone Road, NW1
Tel: (020) 7935 6861

National Maritime Museum
Romney Road
Greenwich, SE10
Tel: (020) 8858 4422

National History Museum
Cromwell Road, SW7
Tel: (020) 7938 9123

Tower Bridge Museum
Tower Bridge, SE1
Tel: (020) 7403 3761

Cinemas

Most UK movie premières are shown in London, usually in Leicester Square. It is not always necessary to book a seat for the cinema (unlike other arts such as theatre or opera), but if there is a popular film showing it always pays to book in advance.

Booking tickets for the cinema is easy. You will need to leave credit card details, your name and the number of seats required and preferred seat locations. Your tickets will be available to collect at the specially designated areas at the cinemas. All cinema programmes are listed in the *Evening Standard, Time Out* and some daily broadsheet newspapers.

Reduced prices can be available for:

- large groups of people
- weekly showing before specified times (to be found locally)
- old age pensioners (OAP)
- families on income support
- students with a valid student card.

ADMIRING THE SIGHTS

There is much to see and admire throughout London and there are many books devoted solely to the subject of sightseeing in the capital. Some of these publications are given at the end of this book. Some of the places to visit in the City are as follows:

The City
Guildhall
Members of the public can visit the Great Hall from Monday–Friday (09.00–16.00). If you would like a guide contact the Keeper's Office, Corporation of London, PO Box 270, Guildhall, EC2P 2EJ. Tel: (020) 7332 1460.

Mansion House
You will need to make an appointment to be shown around. Contact the Principal Assistant to the Lord Mayor, Mansion House, EC4N 8NH.

Bank of England Museum
There are a variety of different presentations available, dependent upon the age group visiting. A one-hour slide show can be seen which covers the history and working of the Bank of England. Contact: Visitors Liaison Group, Secretary's Department HO-P, Bank of England, Threadneedle Street, EC2R 8AH. Tel: (020) 7601 3985.

Baltic Exchange
Small groups which have specific interest in international shipping can visit by appointment only. Contact: The Chief Executive, The Baltic Exchange, St Mary Axe, EC3A 8BH. Tel: (020) 7369 1621.

London Metal Exchange
Groups of no more than 15 people of at least 'A'-level standard can arrange to visit to watch the 'ring' and see the video presentation. Contact: The Marketing Department, The London Metal Exchange, 56 Leadenhall Street, EC3M 7HA. Tel: (020) 7264 5555.

London Commodity Exchange
Educational and business groups are welcome to visit by appointment to view the trading. Contact: Business Development Department, London Commodity Exchange, 1 Commodity Quay, St Katharine's Dock, E1 9AX. Tel: (020) 7481 2080.

West End
There are so many places to visit and adventures to have in London's West End (for suggested books see Further Reading on page 123). A few points to bear in mind:

Timing
There are certain times of year when you will see more than usual:

- visit the City on the day of the Lord Mayor's show, usually the second Saturday in November

- visit Whitehall, which leads from Trafalgar Square to Westminster and the Cenotaph, on Remembrance Sunday (closest Sunday to November 11)

- visit Trafalgar Square on New Year's Eve with all the other revellers

- visit Buckingham Palace during the Changing of the Guard (11.30 every two days, except April–July when it is every day)

- visit Hyde Park on Sunday morning as you could well hear a few speeches from Speaker's Corner

- visit Leicester Square on the night of a movie première and you may see a few famous stars

- Covent Garden is great to visit on a sunny Sunday, as there will be many street performers

- take a London sight-seeing tour at night when the Christmas lights have been switched on.

NIGHTLIFE AT ITS BEST

London has a fantastic nightlife scene. There are plenty of nightclubs and dancing, but nightlife in London includes a wide variety of possibilities:

1. There are many restaurants with music, dancing and cabaret as part of the cost of the meal. Many of London's hotels offer this, as does the famous Stringfellow's nightclub. The latter will waive your entrance fee in exchange for the price of the meal (probably pretty high!) Reservations are essential, as is a large amount money or a flexible credit card.

2. There is a wide selection of gay pub, clubs and restaurants. For full information consult *Gay News*.

3. Sporting nightlife is vast for those who wish to participate or watch sport. There are many pubs and bars with large television screens for watching live football and other sports. In addition, there are many large indoor sports centres with squash, badminton, tennis, table tennis, swimming, bowls, snooker, pool, darts, etc.

4. You can decide on a theme evening or a celebrity-spotting evening. There are many celebrities who live in London or visit London frequently. It's an interesting way to amuse out-of-town

visitors. A few places to consider going to celebrity spot are:

Joe Allen
13 Exeter Street, WC2
Tel: (020) 7836 0651

Langan's Brasserie
7 Stratton Street, W1
Tel: (020) 7493 6437

Stringfellows
16–19 Upper St Martin's Lane, WC2
Tel: (020) 7240 5534

Roof Gardens
99 Kensington High Street W8
Tel: (020) 7937 7994

5. There are organised Night Walks around some of London's more notorious streets. Bearing in mind there is safety in numbers, these walks can include such themes as 'Jack the Ripper', 'Ghosts and Pubs', and 'Sherlock Holmes'. See local press for details.

6. Seeing the sights by night can be wonderful fun. Many of the sights, historic buildings and monuments are lit up at night, making them even more spectacular than in daylight. Tourist buses are available from Leicester Square and it always pays to check the itinerary before booking.

7. Late-night shopping is available in Knightsbridge on Wednesday nights and the West End on Thursday nights.

8. You will find many cinemas and restaurants are open throughout the night.

DEVELOPING HOBBIES

Whatever you enjoy doing in your spare time there will be an opportunity to develop your hobby within London. Here are some of the best ways to find out where you can go:

- your local telephone directory

- volunteers groups

- *Floodlight*, which provides details where classes and groups meet regularly

- sports facilities

- walks.

CONTINUING WITH EDUCATION

London has a tradition of excellent adult-education facilities. Classes are open to everyone and many require no qualifications to enrol. The benefit of this is that the students are from a variety of backgrounds, bringing a wide range of expertise to the classes.

Floodlight is the official guide to all part-time and full-time courses in Greater London. You will find this book in the reference section of all London libraries.

The book covers the following:

- daytime classes
- evening classes
- details of classes all over London
- fees, with possible concessions
- flexible and open learning
- part-time and full-time courses
- learning for people with difficulties and special needs.

Concessions with payments are available to:

1. People receiving state retirement pensions.

2. People registered as unemployed.

3. People receiving income support and other benefits.

CHECKLIST

1. Visit your local library to research background information before buying any books.

2. Accept invitations to visit new venues and areas.

3. Organise your social visits.

10

Practical Information

This chapter aims to give you a few additional hints and tips on behaviours and expectations of living and working in London, from dealing with emergency situations to keeping positive.

TIPPING

When living and working in London you will soon learn that most aspects of any service provided need to be tipped. Many employees in service industries, particularly hotels and catering, expect part of their salary through tips from happy customers and clients. Here are some guidelines to tipping:

- cafés and bars which offer a table-waiting service expect a tip of approximately 10 per cent, even if you only have a cup of coffee (but you don't have to tip a bar person if you order a drink at a bar)
- many of the hotels and nightclubs expect you to leave a tip for the attendant in the toilets and the cloakroom attendant, this can be anything from a few pence up to £1
- drivers of black taxis will expect a tip in the region of 10 per cent of the taxi fare
- restaurants will vary, as some include service on the bill total – up to 15 per cent – whilst others leave any service payment to the discretion of the customer. You should tip what you feel is relevant for the service provided, although a good average is 10 per cent of the total bill
- doormen at hotels and higher-class nightclubs and restaurants are accustomed to being given 50 pence or £1
- hairdressers will expect to be tipped around 10 per cent of the bill.

TELEPHONING HOME

If you have constant access to a telephone in shared accommodation, always ensure that at the outset all the occupants have agreed on how the payment of the telephone bill will be calculated. Remember that if the bill goes even partially unpaid then you may lose the use of the telephone altogether. It's an important point to clarify.

If you do not have the use of a telephone for personal calls, then you may want to invest in one of the following:

1. A mobile telephone may be your best option. Always consult an independent expert who can advise you on the best available option for your specific requirements. A contact number is essential if you are job hunting.

2. Your parents or guardians may provide you with a telephone charge card charged to their own number.

3. You can rely on ordinary telephone cards and loose change. This is probably the most unreliable method, although it usually saves you money on telephone calls.

KEEPING HEALTHY

Here are some hints and tips to keep your new life in London more comfortable:

- look after your health
- take care of yourself when walking around on your own
- venture to new places
- make the most of all opportunities as presented to you
- develop new friendships and relationships
- do not over-spend.

Anyone who has lived in a close-knit community knows what it is like to have everyone knowing and watching your every move, and there are pluses and minuses to this. London cannot be described as a close-knit community in the same way, as everyone has their own lives to live and are often very busy. Generally people do not have the time to take a close interest in anyone else's life. This means that you will be on your own. Naturally this has its advantages and disadvantages.

The advantages of this style of living do not suit everyone. However, those who enjoy this type of freedom can enjoy many things:

- the freedom to come and go as you please without having to explain your every move to anyone
- the opportunity to develop your life and career in the direction you desire without any interference
- the openings to give you the chance to enjoy yourself how you wish
- the ease to change your mind about anything without having to explain your motivations
- the choice to dress exactly as you wish.

On the other hand, you will have to take responsibility for your own health and well-being by being adult and ensuring you always have a fall-back position. While this may sound straightforward, it is an aspect which can easily be overlooked, especially when first moving in. You may feel that you lack time initially, with accommodation and work to be found. Remember that the following are ways to ensure parents, guardians and friends realise you are taking control of your life in a sensible manner. This will keep them happier and less likely to be worried. More importantly it will add to your level of personal safety.

1. One of the first tasks should be to find yourself a doctor and dentist close to where you live or work. You may need other medical specialists if you have a specific illness. The local telephone directory and personal recommendation are the easiest ways to find these professionals. The sooner you organise these the easier it will be when there is a problem.

2. If you believe that you will be spending some time unemployed then you will need to seek out your nearest Department of Social Security. The details of this can be found in the telephone directory under 'Benefits Agency'. The London Emergency

Number is (020) 7401 9692. Once again, the sooner you arrange a visit the sooner you will receive money and understand your position. One point to be aware of is that, in central London, these offices are huge and you can find that it takes a whole morning or afternoon to receive forms and information. This will be followed by a return visit and possibly an interview, which could take another whole morning or afternoon.

3. Accept that the freedom you have been given has a down side to it. You can spend hours, even days or weeks without anyone in London showing any interest in your movements or where-abouts. Consequently it is important that you organise to make a call or visit, at least once a week with a friend or member of the family. You may find it less intrusive if this is a responsible friend, as opposed to a family member. If you cannot make the call or visit, you need to notify the friend. At least one person will know that you are well each week.

4. Keep to a healthy diet with enough exercise. Ensure that even if you enjoy going out to party and stay up all night, you take care of yourself and get enough sleep at other times. If you want a career in London you will need to balance this aspect with care.

5. Avoid sitting at home on your own every night because you are finding London life too exhausting. This can have a destructive effect on your self-esteem. Book yourself into an evening class.

6. Avoid drugs and avoid socialising with anyone who sells or takes drugs.

7. Ensure that you present yourself at work well-dressed, alert and keen, whatever your lifestyle. Being able to choose how to dress does not mean that you can turn up for a job interview with a chartered accountant with torn jeans and purple hair – at least not if you want a job offer!

Benefits of spending time on your own

It may be that during your first few weeks, or even months in London you do not spend much time on your own. You will be keen trying to build up a network of friends as well as visiting the sights.

This makes it even more important to learn how to enjoy your own company. Some of the benefits of time on your own are:

• a chance to relax without interruption

- an opportunity to assess situations and think through solutions
- an occasion to give yourself a treat, something you prefer doing on your own
- an opportunity to catch up on news, both local and from back home
- the time to focus on your own health and well-being
- a chance to rejuvenate.

DEALING WITH EMERGENCIES

In times of trouble you may feel comforted if you know who to call. London life can be stressful enough without adding emergencies to the list. Here are some helpful addresses, telephone numbers and organisations:

Emergencies
Ambulance **999**
Police   **999**
Fire service **999**

Embassies
American: 24 Grosvenor Square, W1. Tel (020) 7499 9000.
Australian: Australia House, Strand, WC2. Tel: (020) 7379 4334.
Canada: Canadian High Commission, 38 Grosvenor Street, W1. Tel: (020) 7409 2071.
New Zealand: 80 Haymarket, SW1. Tel: (020) 7930 8422.

Medical information
Healthline: Tel: 0345 678 444.
Medical Advisory Service: Tel: (020) 8994 9874.

24-hour casualty departments
Charing Cross Hospital, Fulham Palace Road, SW6. Tel: (020) 8846 1234.
Guy's Hospital, St Thomas Street, SE1. Tel: (020) 7955 5000.
Royal London Hospital, Whitechapel Road, E1. Tel: (020) 7377 7000.
University College Hospital, Grafton Way, WC1. Tel: (020) 7387 9300.

Locksmiths
Barry Bros, 121 Praed Street, WC2. Tel: (020) 7734 1001.
Chiswick Security, 4 Denbigh Street, SW2. Tel: (020) 7630 6500.

Helplines
Capital Helpline: Tel: (020) 7388 7575.
Citizens Advice Bureau: Tel: (020) 7251 2000.

LISTENING TO LONDONERS

The best way to get a feel for a country or city is to talk to those who live there – 'when in Rome...' as the saying goes. Here are some insights into what Londoners love about their famous city:

- live jazz at Pizza Express on Dean Street
- the view from Alexandra Palace
- Greenwich Market's jewellery
- walking across London Bridge after dark and seeing St Paul's Cathedral and Tower Bridge lit up
- shopping at Camden Market
- finding your way through the narrow backstreets of Mayfair
- being in Soho or Covent Garden as London comes awake
- walking through Hyde Park with a dog
- trying olives and other delicacies in Selfridge's Food Hall
- going to a movie at Leicester Square on Sunday morning.

Your favourite things are guaranteed to change each week as you discover all that London has to offer.

KEEPING CONFIDENT

Any change of circumstances can undermine your confidence and composure. As discussed before you will have to face new people and new places in a hectic new way of life. One of the most effective ways of keeping your confidence is to ensure that you take charge of situations. Here are some hints and tips:

- assess each situation on merit and analyse the alternatives before making a decision and/or acting on the information
- structure your action plan and steps for the future to give yourself the flexibility to face a variety of different situations
- surround yourself with a positive-thinking group of friends
- be prepared to let go of acquaintances if they constantly put you down or have an unreasonably negative outlook
- practise assertiveness or even go to an assertiveness evening class.

CHECKLIST

1. Organise for telephone calls to be made and received with your house sharers.
2. Action plan your health requirements.
3. Check out who to call in an emergency.
4. Listen to Londoners.

Useful Addresses

GENERAL

City Business Library, 1 Brewer's Hall Garden, off Aldermanbury Square, EC2V 5BX

Reed Employment, Staff Agency, 143 Victoria Street, SW1. Tel: (020) 7834 1801 *www.reed.co.uk*

Westminster Reference Library, 35 St Martin's Street, WC2H 7HP. Tel: (020) 7641 4634

Aliens Registration Office, 10 Lamb's Conduit Street, WC1. Tel: (020) 7230 1208

BUNAC (British Universities North America Camp), 16 Bowling Green Lane, EC1. Tel: (020) 7251 3472.

Central Bureau for Educational Visits and Exchanges, British Council, 10 Spring Gardens, W1. Tel: (020) 7486 5101

Department for Education & Employment, Overseas Labour Service, Level 5, Moorfoot, Sheffield S1 4PQ. Tel: (0114) 259 4074

Home Office, Lunar House, 40 Wellesley Road, Croydon CR9 9BY. Tel: (020) 8686 0688

GENERAL WEB SITES

http://www.hotels-london.de/tourist_info.htm
London Tourist Information: Sightseeing, events, tours, budget accommodation, transport, museums, galleries, internet, theatres, pubs, clubs, restaurants, tickets, flights to London

http://london.eventguide.com/
Annually-recurring events in Greater London in the arts, sporting events, conventions, festivals and parades

http://www.tourist.co.uk
London Tourist Information Service
24-hour tourist information hotline: 0839 33 77 99 (+44 171 244 9999 from outside the UK)

CASUALTY DEPARTMENTS

Charing Cross Hospital, Fulham Palace Road, SW6. (020) 8846 1234
Guy's Hospital, St Thomas Street, SE1. Tel: (020) 7955 5000
Royal London Hospital, Whitechapel Road, E1. Tel: (020) 7377 7000
University College Hospital, Grafton Way, WC1. Tel: (020) 7387 9300

CHEAP EATS

Café Emm, 17 Frith Street, W1. Tel: (020) 7437 0723
Stockpot, 18 Old Compton Street, W1. Tel: (020) 7287 1066
Sausage & Mash, 269 Portobello Road, W6. Tel: (020) 8968 8848

CHURCHES

St Martin-in-the-Fields, Trafalgar Square, WC2N 4JJ. Tel: (020) 7930 0089
  www.stmartin-in-the-fields.org
Westminster Abbey, off Parliament Square. Enquiries to: Chapter's Office,
  20 Dean's Yard, Westminster Abbey, London SW1 3PA Parliament
  Square, SW1. Tel: (020) 7222 5152. *www.westminster-abbey.org*
Westminster Cathedral, Victoria Street, SW1. Tel: (020) 7798 9055.
  www.westminstercathedral.org.uk
St James's Church Piccadilly, 197 Piccadilly, W1. Tel: (020) 7734 4511
All Hallows by the Tower, Byward Street, EC3. Tel: (020) 7481 2928
St Bride's, Fleet Street, EC4. Tel: (020) 7353 1301
St Etheldreda's, Ely Place, EC1. Tel: (020) 7405 1061
Southwark Cathedral, Montague Close, SE1. Tel: (020) 7367 6700.
www.southwark.gov.uk/tourism/attractions/southwark_cathedral

THE CITY

Guildhall, The City of London, EC2P 2EJ. Tel: (020) 7332 1460
Mansion House, Walbrook, ECVN 8BH. Tel: (020) 7626 2500
Baltic Exchange, St Mary Axe, EC3A 8BH. Tel: (020) 7369 1621
London Metal Exchange, 56 Leadenhall Street, EC3M 7HA. Tel: (020) 7264
  5555
London Commodity Exchange, 1 Commodity Quay, St Katharine's Dock,
  E1 9AX. Tel: (020) 7481 2080

EMBASSIES

The American Embassy, 24 Grosvenor Square, W1. Tel: (020) 7499 9000
The Australian Embassy, Australia House, Strand, WC2. Tel: (020) 7379
  4334 *www.australia.org.uk*
The Canadian High Commission, 38 Grosvenor Street, W1. Tel: (020) 7409
  2071
The New Zealand Embassy, 80 Haymarket, SW1. Tel: (020) 7930 8422

LAW COURTS

Gray's Inn, Gray's Inn Road, WC1. Tel: (020) 7458 7800
Lincoln's Inn, Lincoln's Inn Fields, WC2. Tel: (020) 7405 1393
Middle Temple, Middle Temple Lane, EC4. (020) 7427 4800
Inner Temple, Inner Temple Treasury Office, EC4. Tel: (020) 7797 8250

LOCKSMITHS

Barry Bros, 121 Praed Street, WC2. Tel: (020) 7734 1001
Chiswick Security, 4 Denbigh Street, SW2. Tel: (020) 7630 6500

MUSEUMS & GALLERIES

Bank of England Museum, Threadneedle Street, EC2R 8AH. Tel: (020) 7601 5545 *www.bankofengland.co.uk*
Royal Naval College, King William Walk, SE10. Tel: (020) 8858 2154
Museum of Artillery, The Rotunda, Repository Road, SE18. Tel: (020) 8316 5402
National Army Museum, Royal Hospital Road, SW3. Tel: (020) 7730 0717
Geffrye Museum, Kingsland Road, E2 8EA. Tel: (020) 7739 9893 *www.geffrye-museum.org.uk*
Percival David Foundation of Chinese Art, 53 Gordon Square, WC1H 0PD. Tel: (020) 7387 3909 *www.soas.ac.uk*
Museum of Garden History, St Mary-at-Lambeth, Lambeth Palace Road, SE1 7LB. Tel: (020) 7261 1891 *www.museumgardenhistory.org*
Bethnal Green Museum of Childhood, Cambridge Heath Road, E2 9PA. Tel: (020) 8983 5200
Museum of Mankind, 6 Burlington Gardens, W1X 2EX. Tel: (020) 7323 8043
Keats' House, Wentworth Place, Keats Grove, NW3. Tel: (020) 7435 2062
Leighton House Museum, 12 Holland Park Road, W14 8LZ. Tel: (020) 7602 3316
Sir John Soane's Museum, 13 Lincoln's Inn Fields, WC2 3BP. Tel: (020) 7405 2107 *www.soane.org*
William Morris Gallery, Lloyd Park, Forest Road, E17 4PP. Tel: (020) 8527 3782 *www.lbwf.gov.uk/wmg*
British Museum, Great Russell Street, WC1B 3DG. Tel: (020) 7636 1555 *www.british-museum.ac.uk*
National Gallery, Trafalgar Square, WC2N 5DN. Tel: (020) 7839 3321 *www.nationalgallery.org.uk*
National Portrait Gallery, 2 St Martins Place, WC2H 0HE. Tel: (020) 7306 0055 *www.npg.org.uk*
Tate Gallery, Millbank, SW1P 4RG. Tel: (020) 7887 8000 *www.tate.org.uk/London*
Wallace Collection, Hertford House, Manchester Square, W1M 6BN. Tel: (020) 7935 0687 *www.the-wallace-colection.org.uk*
Serpentine Gallery, Kensington Gardens, W2 3XA. Tel: (020) 7402 6075 *www.serpentinegallery.org*
Madame Tussaud's, Marylebone Road, NW1. Tel: (020) 7935 6861
Courtauld Institute of Art, Somerset House, Strand, WC2R 0RN. Tel: (020) 7848 2526 *www.courtauld.ac.uk*
Dulwich Picture Gallery, College Road, SE21 7AD. Tel: (020) 8693 5254
Victoria & Albert Museum, Cromwell Road, SW7 2RL. Tel: (020) 7938 8500 *www.vam.ac.uk*
Imperial War Museum, Lambeth Road, SE1 6HZ. Tel: (020) 7416 5000 *www.iwm.org.uk*

National History Museum, Cromwell Road, SW7 5BD. Tel: (020) 7938 9123 *www.nhm.ac.uk*

Cabinet War Rooms, Clive Steps, King Charles Street, SW1. Tel: (020) 7930 6961 *www.iwm.org.uk*

London Transport Museum, 39 Wellington Street, Covent Garden WC2E 7BB. Tel: (020) 7379 6344 *www.ltmuseum.co.uk*

National Maritime Museum, Romney Road, SE10. Tel: (020) 8858 4422 *www.nmm.ac.uk*

Tower Bridge Experience, Tower Bridge, SE1 2UP. Tel: (020) 7403 3761 *www.towerbridge.org.uk*

NIGHT LIFE

Joe Allen, 13 Exeter Street, WC2. Tel: (020) 7836 0651

Langan's Brasserie, 7 Stratton Street, W1X 5FD. Tel: (020) 7493 6437

Roof Gardens, 99 Kensington High Street, W8 5ED. Tel: (020) 7937 7994

Stringfellows, 16-19 Upper St Martin's Lane, Covent Garden, WC2H 9EF. Tel: (020) 7240 5534 *www.stringfellows.co.uk*

THEATRES

Lyric, King Street, W6. Tel: (020) 8741 2311 *www.lyric.co.uk*

Old Vic Theatre, The Cut, Waterloo Road, SE1 8NB. Tel: (020) 7928 7616

The Mermaid Theatre, Puddle Dock Blackfriars, EC4V 3DB. Tel: (020) 7236 1919 *www.mermaid-theatre.co.uk*

Royal National Theatre, South Bank, SE1 9PX. (020) 7452 3400 *www.nt-online.org*

The Barbican Centre, Box Office, Silk Street, London, EC2Y 8DS. Tel: (020) 7638 8891 *www.barbican.org.uk*

Shakespeare's Globe, New Globe Walk, Bankside, SE1. Tel: (020) 7928 6406

Further Reading

Finding a Job with a Future, Laurel Alexander (How To Books)
Applying for a Job, Judith Johnstone (How To Books)
How to Manage your Career, Roger Jones (How To Books)
Writing a CV that Works, Paul McGee (How To Books)
Buying a House, Adam Walker (How To Books)
Great Answers to Tough Interview Questions, Martin John Yate (Kogan Page)
How the City of London Works, William M Clarke (Sweet & Maxwell)
The Oxford Dictionary of Art (Oxford University Press)
Nicholson *London Museums and Galleries* (Harper Collins)
Time Out books
AA *London All-in–one-guide* (AA Publishing)

NEWSPAPERS AND JOURNALS

Day	Jobs, Careers	Accommodation	Out and About
Monday	*Guardian* *Evening Standard*	*Evening Standard*	
Tuesday	*Guardian* *Independent* *Evening Standard*	*Evening Standard*	
Wednesday	*Guardian* *Evening Standard* *Financial Times*	*Evening Standard* – property day	
Thursday	*Times* *Telegraph* *Evening Standard*	*Evening Standard* *Loot* – weekly	*Time Out* – weekly
Friday	*Evening Standard*	*Evening Standard*	Tickets magazine free with *Evening Standard*
Saturday	*Guardian* – all of week's jobs		*Guardian*
Sunday	*Sunday Times* *Sunday Telegraph* *Observer* *Independent on Sunday*		

Index